CHARMING
SMALL HOTEL
GUIDES

Switzerland
with Liechtenstein

CHARMING
SMALL HOTEL
GUIDES

Switzerland
with Liechtenstein

Edited by Paul Wade & Kathy Arnold

DUNCAN PETERSEN

HUNTER
PUBLISHING INC

300 Raritan Center Parkway,
CN 94, Edison, N.J. 08818

Conceived, designed and produced by
Duncan Petersen Publishing Ltd,
Edited by Team Wade, The Chapter House, Chiswick Mall,
London W4 2PJ

Editors	Paul Wade, Kathy Arnold
Assistant editor	Nicola Davies
Art director	Mel Petersen
Maps	Chris Foley

This edition published in the UK and Commonwealth 1999 by
Duncan Petersen Publishing Ltd,
31 Ceylon Road, London W14 OPY

Sales representation and distribution in the U.K. and Ireland by
Portfolio Books Limited
Unit 1C, West Ealing Business Centre
Alexandria Road
London W13 0NJ
Tel: 0181 579 7748

ISBN 1 872576 76 1

A CIP catalogue record for this book is available
from the British Library

AND

Published in the USA 1994 by
Hunter Publishing Inc.,
300 Campus Drive, Edison, N.J. 08818.
Tel (732) 225 1900 Fax (732) 417 0482

For details on hundreds of other travel guides and language
courses, visit Hunter's Web site at
http://www.hunterpublishing.com

ISBN 1-55650-869-7

Originated by Reprocolor International S.R.I., Milan
Printed by G. Canale & Co SpA, Turin

Contents

Introduction

This is the seventh book in the well-established series of
Charming Small Hotel Guides, in addition to France, Italy,
Spain, the British Isles, Germany and Austria and the USA.
Long one of Europe's most popular tourist destinations
because of its breathtaking mountain scenery, its famous
winter sports resorts and the punctuality of its railways, it
also has beguiling villages and unspoilt countryside.

To enjoy Switzerland to the full, a charming, small,
family-run hotel is essential. Swiss hoteliers have set the
benchmark for hotel-keeping around the world, yet the
spirit of service, cleanliness and welcome springs from
hundreds of years of tradition in wayside inns and village
hostelries.

We have listed 200 small hotels here. Most have fewer
than 30 bedrooms ranging from total luxury to rustic
country simplicity. Some are in cities, others deep in pine
forests; some are on the shores of beautiful lakes, others
surrounded by vines or a few steps from a ski-trail. A few
are extravagantly expensive, others appeal to the budget-
conscious traveller. All are united in offering old-
fashioned, personal hospitality, the comforts demanded by
today's travellers and the willingness to go out of their way
to make the holiday-maker happy.

Hotel, guesthouse, Landgasthof and Relais de Campagne
Under the collective banner of *Charming Small Hotels* we
list all sorts of accommodation. A handful may only
provide bed and breakfast, some concentrate on their
excellent restaurants and offer only a few bedrooms; most
are family-owned with one partner cooking and the other
running the hotel. We have been both impressed and
puzzled by the relatively new label invented by the Swiss
Hotel Association, the *Landgasthof* or *Relais de Campagne*.
At their best, these are old inns, with old furniture and
plenty of character both downstairs and in the bedrooms.
Regional dishes feature in the restaurants and *Stube*. At the
other end of the scale, they can be too simple and basic,
with not enough attention paid to the bedrooms which
are dull and dark. We approve of the concept, but would
welcome a more consistent high standard. We would also
like to see them better signposted .

Selection
This selection of hotels has been made after thorough
research, personal recommendations and expert
inspection by a team of travel-writers who have many
years of experience around the world. **No hotel pays to
be in this guide.**

Introduction

Entries
As in other books in the series, our warmest
recommendations are reflected in full-page reports,
complete with colour photograph. At the back of the book
is a further selection of shorter entries, four to a page.
These are by no means 'second-class' hotels, but for one
reason or another do not justify a full page.

Switzerland's variety
The wide cultural variety in this small, mountainous
country is reflected by the four official languages: French,
German, Italian and Romansch. Not all of the Swiss speak
all four, but most hoteliers speak two, if not three, and
have English as well. There are other regional differences,
too. Our inspectors enjoyed French-influenced cuisine,
German attention to detail, sunshine and warmth in
Ticino and the rich traditions of the Romansch-speakers
in Graubünden, in the east.

Liechtenstein
Often regarded as part of Switzerland, the Principality is
worth visiting in its own right. We found some fine hotels
and restaurants.

Prices
Switzerland enjoys a high standard of living which means
that it is expensive for many visitors. Prices, however,
include all taxes and service charges. Discounts are
available to hotel guests once they commit themselves to
dinner, bed and breakfast for a stay of 3 days or longer.
Always ask about reductions, especially out-of-season, but
don't be surprised to pay as much for a rustic bedroom
with a fabulous view as for a smart bedroom in a city hotel.

Bedrooms
Many of our readers prefer the comfort of their own
separate bed and are keen to know about twin-bedded
bedrooms. In most hotels, the traditional Swiss double bed
is essentially two singles, pushed together, with separate
mattresses and separate duvets. We found that a true
'double bed', called 'a French bed', was a rarity.

Public rooms
In German-speaking Switzerland, the *Stube* is the focal
point of older hotels. Usually beautifully wood-panelled,
this room, with its bench seats, large tables and *Kachelofen*
(ceramic stove) is the place to relax, as well as eat and
drink.
   In the Italian-speaking Ticino, *grottos* are the equivalent,

ready to offer home-made sausage, cheese and wine.

In Romansch, look out for rooms labelled *Stivetta* or *Stüvetta*, the equivalent of a *Stube*.

Meals

Breakfast is usually served spread out, buffet-style, for guests to help themselves. Cereals, fresh and dried fruits, cold meats and cheeses plus a variety of breads or rolls satisfy the heartiest appetites. We would still like to see hotels give more attention to good orange juice and home-made jams. We were disappointed to find that almost all hotels use miserly pre-wrapped pats of butter, yet this is the land famous for its cows, milk and cheese.

Bio

The word *Bio* means 'organic'. Wholefood ingredients are commonly used even though they are not highlighted on menus. Now hoteliers are beginning to realise that guests like to be told which dishes are prepared using organic produce from local farmers.

Smoking

This is still a popular vice. Most hoteliers feel that they would upset guests if they had any sort of smoking ban. Yet the handful that are brave enough to ban smoking tell us that they have few problems. We would like to see more non-smoking areas in dining-rooms, as well as non-smoking bedrooms.

Electricity

Although many hotels have 'international' sockets, we still advise electric razor-users to take adaptors.

Credit cards

Credit cards are in common use, especially since Switzerland has so many business travellers. However, we advise readers to double-check which cards are accepted when making a reservation.

Your host and hostess

Most inn-keepers enjoy being involved with their guests, whether it is cross-country skiing or hiking, tasting wines or teaching cookery. Pleasant as an overnight stay will be, a longer visit will always give added insight into the local family and region.

Introduction

Travel facts
The staff at Switzerland Tourism offices around the world are particularly helpful to the individual traveller when it comes to special interest holidays.

The Switzerland Travel Centre in Britain is at: Swiss Centre, Swiss Court, London W1V 8EE Tel: (0171) 734 1921.

In the United States it is at: 608 Fifth Avenue, New York, NY 10020 Tel: (212) 757 5944 and also 222 No Sepulveda Blvd, Suite 1570, El Segundo, Los Angeles, CA 90245. Tel: (310) 335 5980. Website: www.switzerlandvacation.ch

Regional tourist offices in Switzerland are listed with their relevant maps.

Flights
Switzerland has a network of regional airports serving Basel, Berne, Geneva, Lugano and Zurich. Crossair links Switzerland with 84 destinations in 29 countries, flown by a 77-strong fleet of aircraft including Avro RJ100 Jumbolinos, Saab 2000 Concordinos, and Boeing/McDonnell Douglas jets.

Crossair operates 28 direct daily scheduled flights from the UK and Ireland and Switzerland, including 5 daily flights between London City Airport and Zurich, as well as flights to Lugano, Geneva, and Basel. Flights to the EuroCross hub at EuroAirport Basel Mulhouse Freiburg have convenient onward connections to some 33 European destinations. Flight bookings and other information on the Internet at www.crossair.ch. In the UK, telephone (0345 662233). In the USA (800 435 9792)

Car Hire
Among the many car rental companies in Switzerland, Avis offers comprehensive coverage of the country thanks to its 40 outlets which include offices at 5 airports (Basel, Bern, Geneva, Lugano and Zurich). The Avis SuperValue programme, bookable 14 days in advance, includes unlimited mileage, collision-damage waiver, theft protection insurance and taxes. In the UK, telephone (0990) 900 500. In the USA, toll-free (800) 311 1212.

Travel Passes
The Switzerland Travel Centre has details of many special passes. For example, the Swiss Pass gives unlimited travel on the railways, lakeboats, postal coaches and even on urban transportation in 36 Swiss towns. It also gives a discount on mountain railways and cable-cars. This, along with the Family Card covering children, is an attractive money-saver.

Introduction

How to find an entry

Entries are arranged geographically. Switzerland is divided into four regions: we start in Western Switzerland and move clockwise through Northern and Central, Eastern and Southern Switzerland. Each of our regions consists of sub-divisions with one or more of the 26 cantons. Liechtenstein has a separate entry.

Each area has its own map, with hotel locations marked with page references.

Then come the main, full-page entries, listed in alphabetical order by town. Finally come the shorter, quarter-page entries again in area order, again listed in alphabetical order by town.

There are three easy ways to find a hotel:

Use the maps between pages 14 and 31. The numbers on the map refer to the page in the book where the hotel is listed.

If you know the area you want to visit, browse through that section until you find a place that fits the bill.

Use the indexes at the back which list entries both by hotel name (p155-157) and by location (p158-160).

How to read an entry

At the top of the page is the area of Switzerland; below that is the region; then follows the type of hotel, its town and, finally, the name of the hotel itself.

The snowflake ❊

We have added the snowflake symbol to help you to recognize hotels catering for winter sports.

Fact boxes

Beneath each hotel description are the facts and figures which should help you to decide whether or not the hotel is in your price range and has the facilities you require. Do confirm prices when you make your reservation.

Tel

The first number is the area code used within Switzerland. When dialling from abroad, omit the initial 0 of this code.

Fax

Most hotels now have a fax number which makes reservations swifter, easier and more reliable.

Location

The setting of the hotel is described briefly; car parking facilities follow.

Introduction

Meals
Most hotels offer all meals, even snacks and light meals, but we have also included some quality bed-and-breakfasts, too.

Prices
In this new edition of Switzerland we have coded the prices into bands. These prices range from the cheapest single room in low season to the most expensive double room in high season. Do ask proprietors about special reductions for length of stay, for extra beds in the room, or for children.

S under 100 Swiss francs
SS 100 to 200 Swiss francs
SSS 200-300 Swiss francs
SSSS over 300 Swiss francs

Rooms
We summarize the number and type of bedrooms available. Our lists of facilities in bedrooms do not cover ornaments such as flowers or consumables such as toiletries.

Facilities
We list public rooms as well as outdoor and sporting facilities which are either part of the hotel or close by; facilities in the vicinity of the hotel feature at the end of the main section under **Nearby**.

Credit cards
We use the following abbreviations for credit cards:
AE American Express
DC Diners Club
MC Master Card/Access/Eurocard
V Visa/ Barclaycard/Bank Americard/Carte Bleue

Closed
It is important to double-check with hotels the exact dates of closing between seasons. Good snow conditions, for example, can lengthen a season. The higher mountain resorts do not open for the summer until well into June.

Proprietors
Where managers are employed, we name them.

Introduction

The Swiss Cantons

Switzerland has 26 cantons, each identified in our hotel addresses by their recognised initials.

AG	Aargau	OW	Obwalden
AI	Appenzell	SG	St Gallen
AR }	Appenzell	SH	Schaffhausen
BE	Bern	SO	Solothurn
BL	Baselland	SZ	Schwyz
BS	Baselstadt	TG	Thurgau
FR	Fribourg	TI	Ticino
GE	Geneva	UR	Uri
GL	Glarus	VD	Vaud
GR	Graubünden	VS	Valais
JU	Jura	ZG	Zug
LU	Lucerne	ZH	Zurich
NE	Neuchâtel	FL	Liechtenstein
NW	Nidwalden	CH	Switzerland

Place names

Listed below are some of the common place names that change according to the language in which they are written.

English	French	German	Italian
Aargau	Argovie	Aargau	Argovia
Basel	Bâle	Basel	Basilea
Bern	Berne	Bern	Berna
Fribourg	Fribourg	Freiburg	Friburgo
Geneva	Genève	Genf	Ginevra
Graubünden	Grissons	Graubünden	Grigioni
Lake Geneva	Lac Léman	Genfersee	Lago di Ginevra
Lake Lucerne Cantons	Lac des 4 stättersee	Vierwald- Cantoni	Lago dei 4
Lake Constance	Lac de Constance	Bodensee	Lago di Costanza
Lucerne	Lucerne	Luzern	Lucerna
Matterhorn	Mont Cervin	Matterhorn	Cervino
Neuchatel	Neuchâtel	Neuenburg	Neuchâtel
St Gallen	St-Gall	St Gallen	S Gallo
Solothurn	Soleure	Solothurn	Soletta
Switzerland	Suisse	Schweiz	Svizzera
Ticino	Tessin	Tessin	Ticino
Valais	Valais	Wallis	Vallese
Vaud	Vaud	Waadt	Vaud

Introduction

Glossary of useful terms

French

Addition	bill	*Légumes*	vegetables
Agneau	lamb	*Nouilles*	noodles
Ail	garlic	*Pâte*	pastry, pasta
Biftek	steak		
Boeuf	beef	*Potage*	soup
Canard	duck	*Raclette*	melted cheese on potato
Confiture	jam		
Fondue	melted cheese dip	*Tranche*	slice
Four, au	oven-baked	*Veau*	Veal

German

Braten	roast	*Konditorei*	cake shop
Brot	bread	*Knoblauch*	garlic
Egli	perch	*Nockerln*	dumplings
Ei	egg	*Nudeln*	noodles/pasta
Eintopf	stew	*Rechnung*	bill
Flädle	pancakes	*Rösti*	crisp, fried potatoes
Fleisch	meat		
Forelle	trout	*Spätzli*	special noodles
Gebäck	pastries	*Speck*	bacon
Kachelofen	ceramic heating stove	*Stube, Stübli*	room for eating, drinking
Kalb	veal	*Wasser*	water
Käse	cheese	*Wein*	wine

Italian

Affettato	cold meats	*Fritto*	fried
Affumicato	smoked	*Manzo*	beef
Aglio	garlic	*Pane*	bread
Agnello	lamb	*Panna*	cream
Arrosto	roast (meat)	*Pasticceria*	cake-shop
Bollito	boiled	*Piselli*	peas
Caldo	hot	*Pollo*	chicken
Casalinga	home-made	*Pomodoro*	tomato
Cipolle	onions	*Selvaggina*	game
Conto	bill	*Spiedo, alla*	on a spit
Crudo	raw	*Uova*	eggs
Forno, al	oven-baked	*Vitello*	veal
Freddo	cold	*Zuppa*	soup

Romansch

Acla, acletta	farmhouse	*Grischuna*	Graubünden
Alp	meadow	*Neros*	black
Ava	water	*Paselgia*	church
Bot	hill	*Plaz*	square
Crap	stone	*Senda*	path
Got	wood	*Voa*	street, road

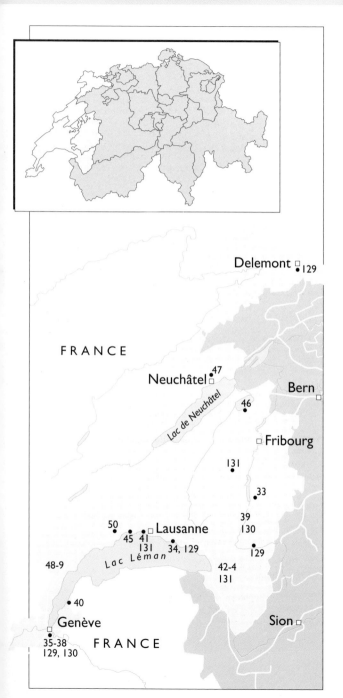

Delemont □ 129

FRANCE

Neuchâtel ● 47
□

Lac de Neuchâtel

Bern □

● 46

□ Fribourg

131
●

● 33

50
●

39
130

45 ● □ Lausanne
41
131

● 129

34, 129

48-9

Lac Léman

42-4
131

● 40

Genève
□
35-38
129, 130

Sion □

FRANCE

Suisse Romande

This is the French-speaking part of Switzerland, bordering France. We have included all but one of the French-speaking cantons in the area: Jura, Neuchâtel, Vaud, Geneva and Fribourg. (Valais has its own section.)

Our inspectors visited some of Switzerland's most cosmopolitan and sophisticated cities, most of which enjoy the balmy climate along Lake Geneva, where vineyards come right down to the water, with the snow-capped mountains as a dramatic backdrop.

We list small hotels both in the middle of Geneva and also in the suburbs, near public transport. There are hotels on hillsides overlooking the lake which are excellent bases for walking or just relaxing. To the north-east in the mountains, and on the smaller lakes further north, are more rural retreats, some quite rustic, others exquisitely-decorated country house hotels.

Our inspectors enjoyed *fondues* made from the region's famous Gruyère cheese. In Fribourg, look for *moitié-moitié* (half-and-half fondues) using Vacherin cheese as well as Gruyère. *Papet*, in the Vaud, is a dish based on sausage and served with leeks, while every menu has freshwater fish from the lakes and streams: *omble chevalier* (char), *perche* (perch) and *truite* (trout). Local wines from La Côte, Lavaux and Chablais are made from the white Chasselas grape. The dry white Dorin from Epesses and the fruitier Dorin from Dézaley are reliable, and an excellent accompaniment for *ramequin*, a Gruyère-flavoured bread pudding.

Union Fribourgeoise du Tourisme
Avenue de la Gare
1701 Fribourg
Tel: (026) 915 9292 Fax: (026) 915 9299
Website: www.pays-de-fribourg.ch

Fédération Neuchâteloise du Tourisme
Hôtel des Postes
2001 Neuchâtel
Tel: (032) 889 6890 Fax: (032) 889 6296

Fédération du Tourisme de la République et du Canton du Jura
Rue de la Gruyère 1
2726 Saignelégier
Tel: (032) 952 1952 Fax: (032) 952 1955

Office du Tourisme du Canton de Vaud
60 Avenue d'Ouchy
1006 Lausanne-Ouchy
Tel: (021) 613 2626 Fax: (021) 613 2600
Website: www.lake-geneva-region.ch

Office du Tourisme de Genève
Rue Mont-Blanc 3
1201 Genève
Tel: (022) 909 7000 Fax: (022) 909 7011
Website: www.geneve-tourisme.ch

Bern

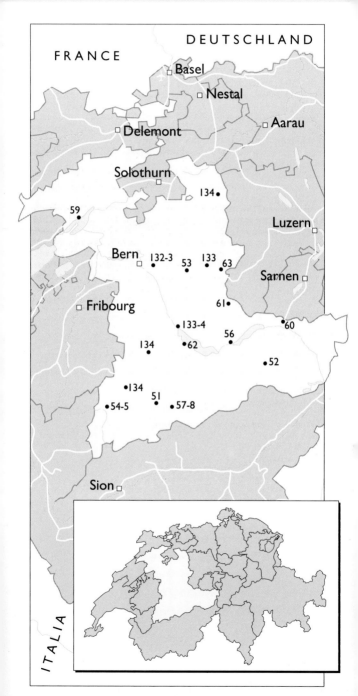

FRANCE

DEUTSCHLAND

□ Basel

□ Nestal

□ Aarau

□ Delemont

Solothurn
□

• 134

59
•

Luzern
□

Bern
□
• 132-3
• 53
• 133
• 63

Sarnen □

□ Fribourg

61 •

• 60

• 133-4

56
•

134
•
• 62

• 52

• 134

51
•
• 57-8

• 54-5

Sion □

ITALIA

Bern

As the second largest canton, Bern can boast many things: the nation's capital, a history older than Switzerland itself and a diverse landscape. Although our inspector found several small hotels on the fringe of the capital, he would have welcomed a high-class small hotel in the old city with its medieval streets and sheltering *Lauben* (arcades) which can be enjoyed in any weather. In fact, to go for a stroll in Bern is referred to as to *laubeln*.

Our inspectors drove the mountain roads to the famous ski resorts in the Bernese Oberland, the region that can justifiably claim to have inspired the popular image of Switzerland thanks to its towering mountains like the Jungfraujoch and Eiger, its nine deep valleys, the thundering waterfalls and calm lakes, such as Thun and Brienz.

Although many of the resorts attract the rich and famous, we have found some small, competitively-priced hotels for both walkers and skiers.

As for food, this is the home of *Rösti*, the flat, crisply-fried potato cake that is now on menus all over the country. There are infinite variations with or without onions, cheese or bacon. Another local dish is the *Berner Platte,* a gastronomic challenge that defeated one of our inspectors: a plate piled high with meat, sausage, sauerkraut and potatoes. More subtle is *Ämmitaler Schöfigs*, a lamb stew, fragrant with saffron. The famous Emmental cheese comes from here, as do meringues. These feather-light confections, delicious with thick cream, are named supposedly for Meiringen. Then there is Sbrinz, a hard Parmesan-like cheese that cooks well and is regarded with awe locally even though it is not well-known outside Switzerland.

Verkehrsverband Berner Oberland
Jungfraustr 38
3800 Interlaken
Tel: (033) 823 0303 Fax: (033) 823 0330
Website: www.berneroberland.com

Verkehrsverband Schweizer Mittelland
Postfach
3001 Bern
Tel: (031) 328 1228 Fax: (031) 311 1222
Website: www.smit.ch

Northern Cantons

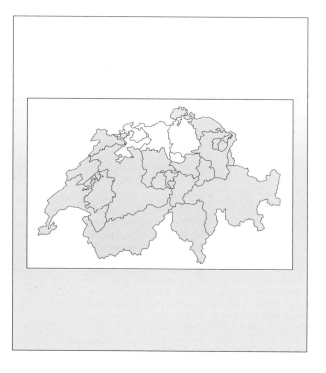

We have lumped together five cantons in this area: Basel and its surrounds, Solothurn, Aargau and Zurich. German is the main language, although Basel draws on influences from France as well as Germany since both countries are just across the border. Basel itself has one of the most astonishing small hotels our inspector has ever seen, while Zurich, Switzerland's largest city, has fine hotels to cater for the international businessmen who wheel and deal here. We like the Savoy Baur en Ville (Poststr 12 Tel: (01) 2152525), a classic example of what Swiss hotel-keeping is all about, even if it is too large for our selection, which includes two very posh lakeside retreats.

Both Basel and Zurich have excellent shops and museums, old architecture and a rich cultural heritage. Another gem is the well-preserved town of Solothurn, which deserves a quality small hotel. As for food, our inspector always loads up with *Basler Leckerli*, the local spiced Christmas cookies, which he much prefers to *Mehlsuppe*, the town's brown soup.

In Solothurn he tried *Saurer Mocken*, at its best a delicious dish of braised beef, served with mashed potatoes or noodles. Although *Geschnetzeltes* appear on menus all over Switzerland, this dish of strips of veal cooked with a mushroom, cream and wine sauce is traditionally associated with Zurich, also the home of Sprüngli's wonderful chocolates and sweets.

Aargau housewives are famous for their *Rüblitorte*, a Swiss-style carrot and almond cake which is lighter than many carrot cakes we have tasted.

Northern Cantons

Verkehrsverein der Stadt Zürich und Umgebung
Bahnhofbrücke 1
8023 Zürich
Tel: (01) 215 4000 Fax: (01) 215 4044
Website: www.zurichtourism.ch

Aargauische Verkehrsvereinigung
Bahnhofstr 50
5400 Baden
Tel: (056) 225318 Fax: (056) 225390
Website: www.baden-schweiz.ch

Verkehrsverein Region Solothurn
Am Kronenplatz
4500 Solothurn
Tel: (032) 626 4646 Fax: (032) 626 4647
Website: www.stadt-solothurn.ch

Basel Stadt/Basel Land
Schifflände 5
4001 Basel
Tel: (061) 268 6868 Fax: (061) 268 6870
Website: www.baseltourismus.ch

Central Cantons

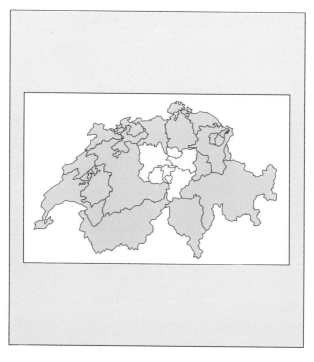

These are not only the geographical hub of Switzerland but also the emotional heart of the country since these German-speaking cantons surrounding the Vierwaldstättersee helped to found the nation some 700 years ago. Here, in the cantons of Lucerne, Zug, Schwyz, Uri, Nidwalden and Obwalden, history is the great attraction: William Tell's shadow falls everywhere.

Mountains like the tall Titlis and the smaller Pilatus, plus the Burgenstock and Rigi are perfect for hiking and winter sports, while the natural beauty of the lakes may be appreciated from the walking trails along the shore, from the steamers that criss-cross the limpid water and from lakeside cafés. Schwyz, which gave its name to Switzerland, is one of several medieval towns that are a delight to visit. That traditional tourist magnet, Lucerne, is still magical despite the tragic fire that destroyed its covered, wooden bridge in 1993, since rebuilt.

On their travels, our inspectors enjoyed some hearty local dishes like the *Luzerner Chügelipastete*, a veal, pork and sausage vol-au-vent with raisins soaked in kirsch. Kirsch also appears in Zug's *Kirschtorte* (cherry cake) where the sponge is soaked in the liqueur. Pears from local orchards are incorporated in *Birnbrot* (pear bread) and *Ziegerkrapfer* (pear fritters).

Verkehrsverband Zentralschweiz
Postfach
6002 Luzern
Tel: (318) 4141 Fax: (318) 4140
Website: www.CentralSwitzerland.ch

Central Cantons

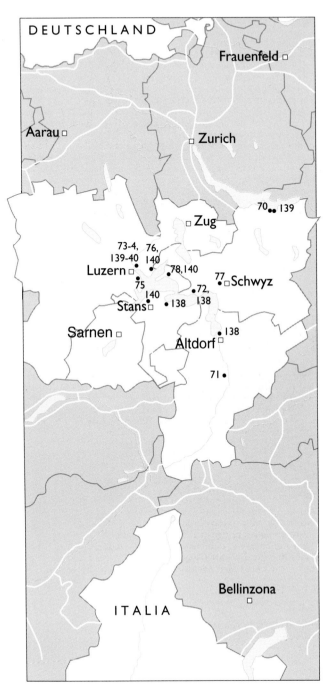

DEUTSCHLAND

Frauenfeld □

Aarau □

Zurich □

70 •• 139

Zug □

73-4, 76,
139-40 140

Luzern □

• 78, 140

77 □ Schwyz

75 •

140 • 72,
Stans □ • 138 138

Sarnen □

• 138

Altdorf □

71 •

Bellinzona □

ITALIA

North-eastern Cantons

Again, we have created our own loose confederation, joining half a dozen cantons together: Schaffhausen, Thurgau, St Gallen, Glarus and Appenzell, which is in turn, made up of two 'half-cantons', Inner and Ausser Rhoden.

These stretch from the south shore of Lake Constance, south to the Alpine pastures of Appenzell with its picture-postcard views of contented cows, rich meadows, gaily-painted houses and, inevitably, snow-capped peaks. Lake Constance itself is rich with wildlife and has many ancient villages along the shore. Schaffhausen, with its medieval guildhalls, is on the Rhine, near the famous Rhine Falls.

Not surprisingly, our inspectors ate lots of fish here, mostly from Lake Constance and all of it carefully prepared, especially the delicate filets of *Egli* (perch). Up on the Appenzell plateau, dishes are heartier. Seek out the mature and very smelly Appenzell cheese, the *Rässkäse,* or, if you have a sweet tooth, ask for *Biberli,* spicy, honey-flavoured cookies. Down in St Gallen the delicacy is the town's famous *Bratwurst* (veal sausage), best eaten with onions and *Rösti,* and accompanied by cider from the abundant orchards of Appenzell.

Thurgau's contribution to the menu is *Tilsiter* cheese, which comes in three degrees of maturity. The best restaurants offer the gold, rich and deeply-flavourful; red-wrapped is medium-strong, while the green *Tilsiter* is quite mild. Thurgau's apples are used in a wide range of tarts but, best of all, in a delicate apple sponge cake.

Tourismus Verband Ostschweiz
Bahnhofplatz 1a
9001 St Gallen
Tel: (071) 227 3737 Fax: (071) 227 3767
Website: www.ostschweiz-i.ch

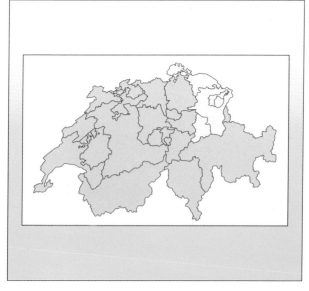

North-eastern Cantons

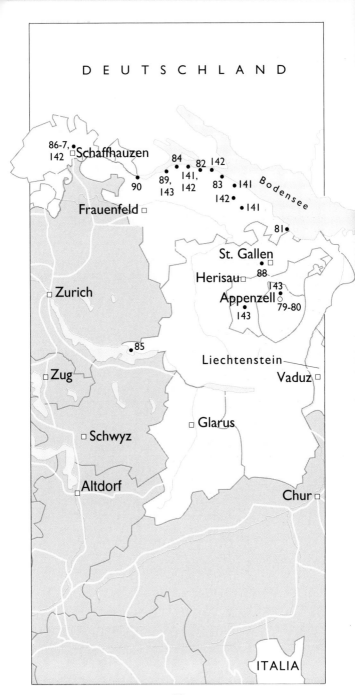

Liechtenstein

DEUTSCHLAND

Bodensee

St. Gallen

Herisau

Appenzell

ÖSTERREICH

Liechtenstein

144

91-3

Vaduz

144

144

144

Chur

Liechtenstein

Liechtenstein is tiny, a mere 25 km by 6 km, yet this principality has a character all of its own. Founded back in 1719 when Schellenberg and the county of Vaduz were merged, this independent country is headed by Prince Hans-Adam II, who lives in the castle overlooking Vaduz and rules over 30,000 people who speak a German dialect. The police force now numbers 50.

There is a surprising amount of open space, with mountains stretching to over 2,500 m and well-marked hiking trails. In summer, picnics and walks in the forests are popular, as is fly-fishing. In winter, the ski resort of Malbun has a wide range of downhill runs, while the nearby Valŭna Valley has machine-set trails for cross-country skiers.

Liechtensteiners are passionate about their wines, which are mainly grown as a hobby. However, there is a small commercial production: *Beerli* is the local Pinot Noir, *Süssdruck* is a young, deep pink wine, sweet, sparkling and fun (also known as *Kretzer*), while the Riesling/Sylvaner is the ubiquitous white grape that enjoys the lime soil of the Principality.

Our inspectors found several top quality restaurants and hotels here.

Liechtensteinische Fremdenverkehrszentrale
Städtle 37
9490 Vaduz
Tel: (0423) 392 1111 Fax: (0423) 392 1618

Please note that 0423 is Liechtenstein's new international code (from 1999).

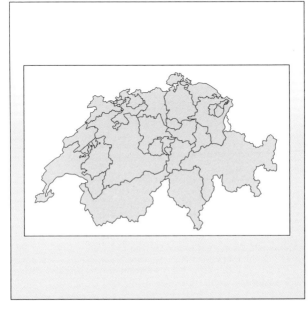

Graubünden

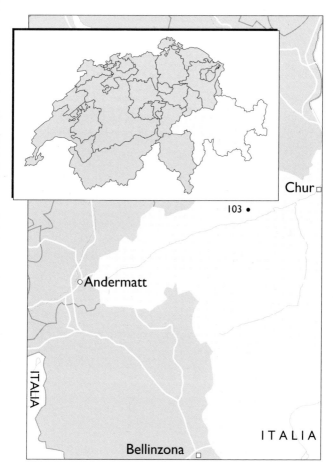

This is the largest canton in the country, a mountainous chunk of eastern Switzerland, with the Engadine, the deep valley of the Inn River, cutting through it from west to east. With Austria to the north and Italy to the south, the area has strong influences from both. It is here that 50,000 inhabitants still speak Romansch, a linguistic legacy of the Roman Empire that is at once familiar and incomprehensible.

Thankfully, despite the importance of tourism, the traditional cattle with their sonorous bells are still part of the landscape, still moved from valley to mountain pasture in spring and back again in autumn. In fact, one of the most unusual and delightful hotels of all was built round a farmyard outside Lenzerheide.

Our inspectors visited famous ski resorts like St Moritz, Davos, Klosters and Arosa, but found the most charming hotels in the villages of the Engadine Valley. Some of Switzerland's finest chefs work here. The Engadine has a tradition of fine *patissiers*, dating back to pastry chefs who came from Venice centuries ago.

Graubünden

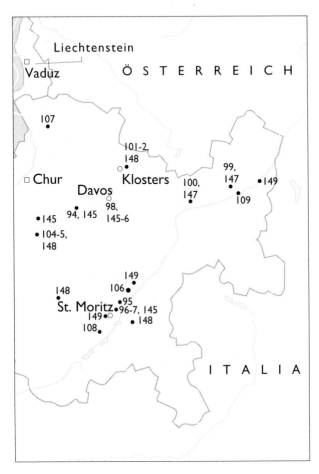

Liechtenstein

Vaduz

ÖSTERREICH

107

Chur

101-2, 148

Klosters

Davos

98, 145-6

94, 145

145

104-5, 148

99, 147

100, 147

149

109

149

106

148

St. Moritz

95

96-7, 145

149

148

108

ITALIA

Nusstorte (nut cake) is a delicacy and each family has a treasured recipe. Other specialities relished throughout Switzerland are the paper-thin slices of *Bündnerfleisch*, air-dried beef that is eaten with the excellent bread or, if you are lucky, added to *Bündner Gerstensuppe*, a rich vegetable soup thickened with pearl barley. Game, especially venison, is popular in the autumn. Our inspectors were served *Pizokels*, pasta made from buckwheat, the equivalent of *Spätzli* or *Knöpfli* elsewhere in Switzerland. They even came across *Strudel*, with different fruit fillings, emphasising the closeness to Austria.

Verkehrsverein Graubünden
Alexanderstr 24
7001 Chur
Tel: (081) 254 2424 Fax: (081) 254 2400
Website: www.graubuenden.ch

Valais

This large, mountainous canton is French-speaking, and, in fact, once belonged to France. Traditionally one of the poorer areas, its inhabitants trekked away to settle elsewhere. Centuries later, these 'Wallisers' are still tightly-knit communities in the Kleinwalsertal of Austria, in Italy and elsewhere in Switzerland. Look for their traditional *mayen* or *mazot* (wooden barns) with distinctive carved wood.

Nowadays, ski resorts on either side of the Rhône Valley attract tourists up the twisting roads. Hotels are used to dealing with the mass market, so small, first-rate hotels are few and far between. Those our inspectors discovered are, however, of a very high standard. We have also included some friendly family-oriented inns where the cheerful atmosphere is ideal for parents and children to relax informally.

Synonymous with the Valais is *raclette*, Bagnes cheese melted by the fire and scraped off, served with boiled potatoes and tart gherkins. Equally hearty fare is the simple *pain de seigle* (rye bread). Local dishes depend on simple ingredients like

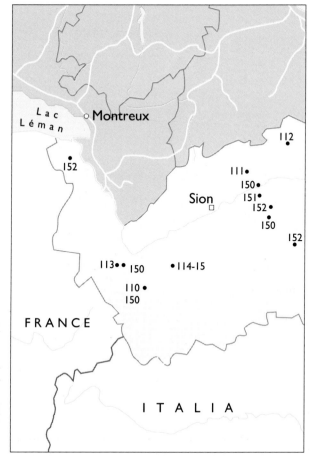

Valais

mushrooms and chestnuts, mountain cheeses and fish from the streams.

The Valais is also a large wine-growing region whose vineyards in the Rhône Valley between Brig and Martigny send Fendant and Dôle all over Switzerland. Fendant is a white wine made from the Chasselas grape; Dôle is red, a blend of Gamay and Pinot Noir. There are also traditional local grape varieties which are still grown. Although not impressive in international terms, it is still fun to try Amigne, Païen, Humagne and Arvine (white) or Goron (red). The Domaine du Château d'Or is, perhaps, the best wine estate in the region.

Union Valaisanne du Tourisme
6 rue Pré-Fleuri
1951 Sion 1
Tel: (027) 327 3570 Fax: (027) 327 3571
Website: www.valaistourism.ch

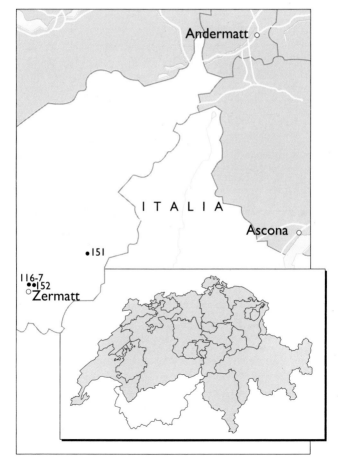

Ticino

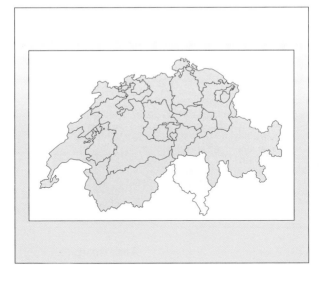

This is the canton that takes first-time visitors by surprise. On the warm, southern side of the Alps, this is Switzerland's Italian-speaking region, with all the blessings of both Italy and Switzerland: mountains and lakes, sunshine and flowers.

Our inspection team found that hotels reflect this Mediterranean feel, with simpler furnishings, many sun-terraces and balconies, but still that Swiss passion for quality, cleanliness and efficiency.

Most of our hotels are on, or overlook, the spectacular lakes of the region, Lugano and Maggiore. Many attract golfers to the nearby courses, while some, with their lush gardens, are particularly romantic. Although Bellinzona is the capital of the canton, Lugano is the focus of the area, combining a bustling old heart, a beautiful lakeside location and thriving financial institutions – all within easy reach of the open countryside.

When it comes to food, the Italian influence is also strong. Home-made *pasta* is regarded as normal; *polenta* (cornmeal) accompanies many dishes; *grappa* (brandy) flavours others; and sausages abound, from the *salamis* for slicing to eat with wine and cheese in a *grotto* (like a pub) to the *luganighe* for grilling over wood. *Risotto* and *pizza* may be common, but are usually delicious. Fish comes from the lakes, grilled or marinaded as a starter; tripe is the flavouring in a vegetable soup called *busecca alla Ticinese.*

Not surprisingly, wine is important and the quality, like the prices, is surprisingly high. Merlot grapes thrive in the southern part of the canton and the rich, red wine accompanies most dishes.

Ente Ticinese per il Turismo
Villa Turrita
6501 Bellinzona
Tel: (091) 825 7056 Fax: (091) 825 3614
Website: www.tourism-ticino.ch

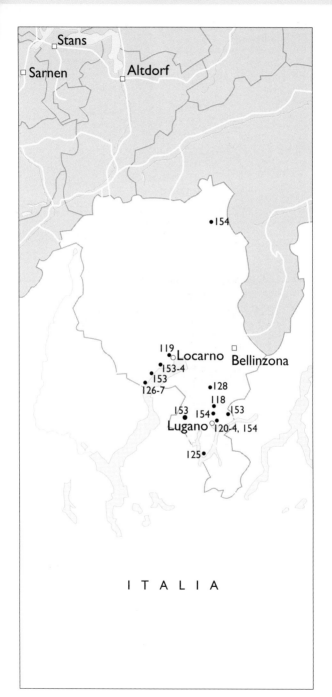

Stans

Sarnen   Altdorf

•154

119
○ Locarno
•153-4   □
•153   Bellinzona
126-7

•128
118
153 154 • •153
Lugano ○ 120-4, 154

125•

I T A L I A

Information

Mountain passes
Switzerland's passes are as famous as the mountain ranges they cross. We list 23 that are open only part of the year; dates are approximate depending on weather conditions.

Mountain	Open
Ächerli	May to Oct
Albula	June to Nov
Chasseral, col de	June to Oct
Croix, col de la	May to Nov
Furka	June to Oct
Glaubenberg	April to Nov
Glaubenbüelen	May to Oct
Grimsel	June to Oct
Ibergeregg	March to Dec
Klausen	June to Oct
Lukmanier	May to Nov
Marchairuz	April to Dec
Nufenen	June to Sept
Oberalp	June to Oct
Planches, col des	June to Oct
S Bernardino, passo del	June to Oct
S Gottardo, passo del	May to Oct
St-Bernard, col du grand	June to Oct
Sanetsch	June to Oct
Splügen	May to Oct
Susten	June to Oct
Umbrail	June to Oct
Weissenstein	April to Dec

Reporting to the guides
Please write and tell us about your experiences of small hotels, guest-houses and inns, whether good or bad, whether listed in this edition or not. As well as hotels in Switzerland, we are interested in charming small hotels in: Britain, Ireland, Italy, France, Spain, Portugal, Germany, Austria and other European countries, as well as the east and west coasts of the United States.

The address to write to is:
The Editors
Switzerland
Charming Small Hotel Guides
Duncan Petersen Publishing Ltd.
31 Ceylon Road
London W14 0PY
England

We assume that in writing you have no objection to your views being published unpaid, either verbatim or in an edited version. Names of major outside contributors are acknowledged in the guide, at the editor's discretion.

Suisse Romande

Le Vieux Chalet

In this part of Switzerland there is a very famous folk song called 'Le Vieux Chalet'. This chalet looks old but was only built in 1960. Does it matter whether or not it is truly ancient? 'No,' decided our reporter. 'After all,' he wrote, 'the ambience in this hugely popular restaurant is certainly Swiss, with open fireplaces plus wood panels and beams, carved doors and chairs. The food, too, is genuine, with favourites such as fondue, *rösti*, trout and *crème de la Gruyère*.' Add in the reasonable prices, making these some of the best value meals to be found in this country, and he was not surprised to find the place full of locals and tourists alike.

'Don't let that put you off,' he advised, 'it is worth coming here just for the exceptional view.' From this hilltop vantage point, you can sit on the terrace and look up towards the Jaunpass, down to the lake, and far along the valley to Gruyères. Stay the night and the silent panorama is all yours. Upstairs, the few rooms are simply furnished, with comfortable beds, old furniture, cheerful red curtains and small shower rooms. Our inspector arrived on Mother's Day, one of the busiest days of the year, and was still given a warm welcome; true Swiss hospitality.

Nearby Gruyères; winter sports.

1653 Crésuz FR
Tel (026) 9271286
Fax (026) 9272286
Location near village of Crésuz; ample car parking
Meals breakfast, lunch, dinner, snacks
Prices rooms S-SS with breakfast
Rooms 3 double; 2 single; all have shower, central heating, TV, radio
Facilities 2 dining-rooms; terrace, garden

Credit cards AE, MC, V
Children very welcome
Disabled not suitable
Pets accepted
Closed Jan; restaurant only, Tues
Languages English, French, German
Proprietors Sudan family

Suisse Romande

Auberge du Raisin

'A model, what hotels should be but rarely are. Gilded grapes hang outside, while the interior looks like a well-kept church, with stone floors, large, simple furniture and wooden ceilings.' Our inspector had nothing but praise for this member of the Relais & Châteaux group, noting that the building dates from the 13thC but bedrooms were recently renovated. 'Flowers are everywhere, not in formal arrangements, but looking as if they have just been brought in from the garden. A vase of asters or poppies brightens the bedrooms, named for people with a Swiss connection, such as Chaplin, Rousseau, Dali, or Stravinsky.' All are beautifully furnished with eye-catching artwork and antique furniture. 'If you can't stay long enough to try them all, try one at the top under the ceiling joists, one with a four-poster bed or, in chilly weather, one with a wood burning stove.' There is no garden but the terrace above the dining-room is peaceful enough for birds to nest in the bay tree. Dutch chef Adolf Blokbergen's cooking is notable: wild duck with a blackcurrant sauce, *rouget* (red mullet) with tiny vegetables *en papillote* and, to finish, apple *beignets* (fritters) with a ginger sauce.

Nearby lake, Lavaux vineyards.

1 place de l'Hôtel-de-Ville, 1096 Cully VD
Tel (021) 7992131
Fax (021) 7992501
E-mail raisin@relaischateaux.fr
Location on main square; car parking on street
Meals breakfast, lunch, dinner, snacks
Prices rooms SS-SSSS (breakfast extra); reduction for children; meals from SF55
Rooms 9 double; 1 single; all have bath or shower, central heating, phone, TV, radio, minibar, hairdrier
Facilities 3 dining-rooms, bar, lift/elevator; terrace
Credit cards AE, DC, MC, V
Children very welcome
Disabled limited access
Pets accepted
Closed never
Languages English, French, German, Italian, Spanish
Manager Adolf Blokbergen

Suisse Romande

City hotel, Geneva

Hôtel les Armures

Although this hotel is only 18 years old, the café next door is the oldest in Geneva and a local institution, where road sweepers lunch inexpensively alongside antique dealers. Upstairs, the restaurant is grander. A full suit of armour stands guard over businessmen, as well as singers from the nearby opera, who order up Swiss and, particularly Genevois, specialties. The buildings date back to the 13thC but the conversion of upstairs rooms into a hotel uncovered beautiful 17thC painted wooden ceilings and ancient walls. Tapestries and old paintings plus well-worn furniture keep the 20thC at bay, although the marble bathrooms have modern conveniences such as shaving mirrors and telephones. Our inspector approved of the subtle inclusion of minibars – hidden in antique bureaux.

Open the windows looking on to the traffic-free old town, smell the fresh flowers in every room (in contrast to the plastic ones in the hallway) and breathe in Geneva. One word of warning: it is easy to get lost in the labyrinth of narrow streets in this part of the city, so take a taxi or follow the map which is faxed out with all reservations.

Nearby Cathedral, Town Hall, Arsenal, Tavel House.

1204 Geneva, rue Puits-St-Pierre 1 GE
Tel (022) 3109172
Fax (022) 3109846
E-mail armures@span.ch
Location in old town pedestrian area; car parking by hotel porter
Meals breakfast, lunch, dinner, snacks
Prices rooms SSS-SSSS with breakfast
Rooms 20 double; 4 single; 4 suites; all have bath or shower, central heating, phone, TV, radio, minibar, hairdrier, air-conditioning
Facilities dining-room, sitting-room, bar, lift/elevator; terrace **Credit cards** AE, DC, MC, V **Children** welcome
Disabled some access
Pets accepted
Closed never
Languages English, French, German, Italian
Proprietors Nicole Borgeat-Granges

Suisse Romande

Auberge de Pinchat, Carouge near Geneva

Daniel Ficht is so busy in his restaurant that he does not have time for guidebook inspectors. His duty, he says, is to the kitchen so he can concentrate on preparing the best food for his guests. With only five bedrooms, advance booking is a must; ask for one away from the road and you will have a perfectly acceptable, if small, place to sleep with good firm beds and a utilitarian bathroom.

Hard at work in the kitchen, Daniel Ficht conjures up delicacies, particularly with fish, to be served in the spacious restaurant, where white walls and linen plus quarry-tiled floor lend an airy, Mediterranean look. Just by the front door is a display cabinet stocked with kitchen products for purchase. Stay the night and you can sample some of the home-made jams and preserves for breakfast, accompanied by that rare find on any hotel breakfast-table, freshly-squeezed orange juice.

As our inspector was departing, he noticed a pool of oil underneath his car. At once, Daniel Ficht produced a can of oil and directions to the local garage. True hospitality from a man who hates guidebook inspectors.

Nearby Mont Salève, Geneva and lake.

1227 Carouge, chemin de Pinchat 33 GE
Tel (022) 3423077
Fax (022) 3002219
Location in country, on edge of town of Carouge; ample car parking
Meals breakfast, lunch, dinner, snacks
Prices rooms SS-SSS with breakfast
Rooms 4 double; 1 single; all have bath or shower, central heating, phone, TV, radio, hairdrier
Facilities dining-room; terrace, garden
Credit cards MC, V
Children welcome
Disabled not suitable
Pets accepted
Closed mid-Aug to early Sept; restaurant only, Sun, Mon
Languages some English, French, Italian
Proprietors Ficht family

Suisse Romande

Village inn, Confignon, Geneva

Auberge de Confignon

The setting is almost perfect: on the corner of a traffic-free village green with a fountain, flowers and views over Geneva and the mountains of the Salève. It even has the village church nearby. Yet this idyll is so close to the city that the number 2 trolley bus stops just at the end of the road, so guests can become temporary commuters, returning each evening to rural peace broken only by the church clock chiming. Donato Farina is a local and very proud of this community of 2,000 inhabitants. Ten years ago he bought this *auberge* and, not content with being the owner, also cooks, producing dishes that often have an Italian flavour.

Do not be put off by the unpromising exterior. Our inspector felt at home as soon as he walked in via the kitchen to the bar. This is the focal point of the hotel and of the village, where business is done and the conversation is animated. Donato is not one for fussiness so bedrooms have a Scandinavian look: white with touches of colour, the occasional print, plenty of potted plants and large cupboards for clothes. Bathrooms are functional. In 1997, the number of rooms doubled when a complete floor was redecorated. Useful base for sightseeing.

Nearby Mont Salève, Geneva and lake, airport.

1232 Confignon, Place de l'Eglise 6 GE
Tel (022) 7571944
Fax (022) 7571889
Location in small village; ample car parking
Meals breakfast, lunch, dinner, snacks
Prices rooms SS with breakfast
Rooms 14 double; all have bath or shower, central heating, phone, TV, radio
Facilities dining-room, bar; garden
Credit cards MC, V
Children welcome
Disabled not suitable
Pets accepted
Closed never; restaurant only, Sun eve, Mon
Languages English, French, German, Italian, Portuguese, Spanish
Proprietor Donato Farina

Suisse Romande

Country hotel, Satigny

Domaine de Châteauvieux

The mass of French cars and international business executives
who regularly find their way to this old stone farmhouse, perched
on a hill top, attest to the fine cooking of Philippe Chevrier. He
and his wife, Bettina, are passionate about their business and set
themselves extremely high standards. Our inspector was relieved
to discover that they have neither been overwhelmed by the
expense account gourmet dining nor fallen prey to the pursuit of
yet more Michelin stars.

The place has a rustic feel with wooden beams, stone floors,
and a courtyard. Our man relished gem after gem from the
kitchen, each course matched by wine produced by vineyards visible from the window. 'This is not the paid-to-smile brigade,' he
wrote in tribute to the staff, 'they really hope you enjoy every
mouthful.' There are rooms as well, furnished in rather plain, traditional style; some have large windows overlooking the Rhône
River and surrounding forests. The bountiful breakfast tempted
our reporter to indulge once more. 'All this and only a short drive
from Geneva and its airport,' he concluded. 'The only thing that
will get thinner if you stay here is your wallet.'

Nearby vineyards, Geneva (10 km), Geneva airport.

1242 Satigny, Peney-Dessus
GE
Tel (022) 7531511
Fax (022) 7531924
Location deep in vineyards,
on hillside overlooking
Rhône; ample car parking
Meals breakfast, lunch,
dinner
Prices rooms SS-SSS with
breakfast
Rooms 17 double; 1 single; all
have bath or shower, central
heating, phone, TV, radio,
minibar
Facilities dining-room; terrace
Credit cards AE, MC, V
Children welcome
Disabled not suitable
Pets accepted
Closed Christmas and New
Year; 2 weeks in Aug;
restaurant only, Sun, Mon
Languages English, French,
German, Italian
Proprietors Chevrier family

Suisse Romande

Hostellerie des Chevaliers

Gruyères is a fixture on the tourist trail and car access is restricted; mention that you are staying at the Chevaliers, however, and the barricade is lifted. Even so, it took our inspector half an hour to find the entrance, outside the old town wall and behind a small car park to the right of the main gate. In 1998, the Corboz family took charge of the family hotel after a 20-year absence. The result is a lighter, brighter and more cheerful ambience. It's a real family affair, with Madame Corboz's son-in-law running the kitchen, where a gastronomic menu complements the traditional fondues and raclettes.

Tiled floors, painted beams and old furniture create a traditional look and you can learn the history of Gruyères from the tapestry in one of the three dining-rooms. An underground passageway hung with pictures links the main villa and another, which houses the bedrooms. These all have stunning views of meadows and mountains with attractive antique Swiss furniture, while bathrooms have received a welcome facelift. This is ideal for families and those wanting to enjoy the medieval town once the tourists have left.

Nearby medieval town of Gruyères; walking; winter sports.

1663 Gruyères FR
Tel (026) 9211933
Fax (026) 9212552
E-mail hotel-chevaliers@bluewin.ch
Location near main gate; car access limited to hotel guests
Meals breakfast, lunch, dinner, snacks
Prices rooms SS-SSS with breakfast
Rooms 28 double; 2 single; 2 family; all have bath or shower, central heating, phone, TV, radio, minibar

Facilities 3 dining-rooms, sitting-room, lift/elevator; terrace, garden
Credit cards AE, DC, MC, V
Children welcome
Disabled suitable
Pets accepted
Closed mid-Jan to mid-Feb; restaurant only, Wed; also Tues in low season
Languages English, French, German
Proprietor Antoine Corboz

Suisse Romande

Country inn, Hermance

Auberge d'Hermance

This is one of those special little places you don't even tell your friends about. Although Hermance has more art galleries than most cities and one or two touristy shops, it retains the character of a village and has successfully fought off too many trappings of the 20thC. The *auberge* describes itself as 'rustic' and rustic it certainly is: there is not a straight line in the place. In the restaurant, wreaths of wheat and and loaves of bread are mixed with wooden ceilings and country prints in a style that would have made Laura Ashley feel at home. Even in spring, it looks autumnal, thanks to the wood fire that burns all year long.

A suite up in the eaves boasts its own fireplace and a bedroom extends the full width of the house with small windows through which you can look out over chimney pots. Paintings are everywhere, which is not surprising since there is an art gallery in the basement.

Here you eat well (*poulet au gros sel* is the speciality) and since there is space upstairs for only three bedrooms plus two suites, you feel as though you are staying with a friend. Book early, particularly on summer weekends.

Nearby medieval village on lake, French border.

Rue du Midi 12, 1248
Hermance GE
Tel (022) 7511368
Fax (022) 7511631
E-mail auberge.dhermance@infomaniak.ch
Location on quiet side-street in old village north-east of Geneva on the lake; car parking in street
Meals breakfast, lunch, dinner, snacks
Prices rooms SF90-250 with breakfast; meals from SF40
Rooms 3 double; 2 suites; all have bath or shower, central heating, phone, TV, radio
Facilities dining-room; terrace, garden
Credit cards AE, DC, MC, V
Children welcome
Disabled not suitable
Pets accepted
Closed never; restaurant only, Tues; Wed in winter
Languages English, French, German, Italian
Proprietor Franz Wehren
Manager Antonio Manteigas

Suisse Romande

Suburban hotel, St Sulpice near Lausanne

Pré Fleuri

Any hotel that quotes Oscar Wilde in its brochure must be worth a visit and our inspector thought the sentiments particularly appropriate for those on holiday with their loved ones: 'After a good meal one bears no grudge against anybody, not even one's own family.' Marie-Odette von Büren proves that a woman can manage a Swiss kitchen, providing splendid French food in the small dining-room or out under the stars in the garden, fragrant with flowers.

This must be the only hotel in this part of Switzerland without a view of the lake and, although situated on a crossroads, there is little sound of traffic. All bedrooms, whether in the original house or the modern annexe, overlook the garden at the back and most have balconies with cheerful striped sunshades. Not surprisingly, those in the old building have more atmosphere but overall, furnishings are unexceptional. In this case, our reporter did not mind: 'Just give me the comfortable beds, the peace and quiet and the sunlight streaming in though open windows. I don't even mind the small bathrooms. No wonder guests return again and again to this quiet oasis.'

Nearby lake, university, ferry; tennis, golf.

rue du Centre 1, 1025 Saint-Sulpice (Lausanne) VD
Tel (021) 6912021
Fax (021) 6912020
E-mail prefleuri@planetmail.com
Location 6 km from Lausanne on Lausanne-Geneva lake road; ample car parking
Meals breakfast, dinner,
Prices rooms SS-SSS with breakfast
Rooms 17 double; all have bath or shower, central heating, phone, TV, radio, minibar
Facilities dining-room; terrace, garden, swimming-pool
Credit cards AE, DC, MC, V
Children very welcome
Disabled not suitable
Pets accepted
Closed Nov to Apr
Languages English, French, German
Proprietors von Büren family

Suisse Romande

⁂ Chalet hotel, Montreux at Caux ⁂

Hostellerie de Caux

If Heidi's grandfather had run a hotel, it would have looked like this. Perched on the mountain, the Hostellerie de Caux is 1,165 m, or more than 20 hair-pin bends, up the steep road from Montreux. Those in the know, however, take the small, blue cogwheel train to the Rochers de Naye. The stop at Caux is just a three-minute walk from the inn. Although popular for weekend lunches in the 1930s, the standards had fallen, as had its reputation, in recent years. Then Jean-Pierre Fath and his Austrian wife decided to escape from Montreux. Formerly a manager of one of the city's large hotels, he left the books and now cooks (fillet of sea trout with chives or lamb with *fines herbes)* to satisfy the hearty appetites of guests who ski in winter and march along the mountain tracks in summer.

Every bedroom has spectacular mountain views, which make up for the rather basic furnishings, although there are comfortable double beds. Bathrooms are small but perfectly adequate. After all, who wants to spend time upstairs when downstairs there is a roaring fire and a bar with a panorama of Lac Léman, the sunset and birds swooping below.

Nearby winter sports; hiking.

1824 Caux-sur-Montreux VD
Tel (021) 9637608
Fax (021) 9632500
E-mail hostelcaux@swissonline.ch
Location above Montreux; cogwheel train stop Hauts-de-Caux; by car, 20 min drive; ample car parking
Meals breakfast, lunch, dinner, snacks
Prices rooms S-SS with breakfast
Rooms 4 double; all have bath or shower, central heating; 2 single with shared facilities
Facilities dining-room, sitting-room with bar; terrace
Credit cards AE, MC, V
Children very welcome.
Disabled not suitable
Pets accepted
Closed mid-Dec to mid-Jan; restaurant only, Thurs, except June to Aug
Languages English, French, German.
Proprietors Thérèse and Jean-Pierre Fath

Suisse Romande

Restaurant with rooms, Clarens near Montreux

L'Ermitage

'Most people come here for the food, among the best in the west
of Switzerland; some come for the art on the walls; others turn off
the busy route 9 for the calm of the lake. I'd come for a bath.'
That bath is in the suite, standing in splendour upon a plinth:
'behind is a potted palm tree; look straight ahead, as you slide
into the bubbles, to the lake with the snow-capped Mont Blanc
framed in the window'. Dragging himself away from that panorama, our man inspected the other bedrooms. Plain walls, lacquered cane furniture and even the large prints blend with colour
schemes such as buttercream and moss-green or tones of pink. All
have welcoming fruit and flowers; five have balconies.

First and foremost, however, is the restaurant. Stylishly modern,
like the bedrooms, it boasts distinctive *trompe-l'oeil* wall paintings.
The Krebs have been here since 1990 and each year the food
seems to get better. Local ingredients feature in dishes such as
rabbit in a sumptuous terrine with *foie gras* or lake trout with a
sauce of two types of parsley. Follow those with a decadent dessert
of almond and chocolate 'cigarettes' with chestnut cream, served
on a black plate. What a picture.

Nearby lake, Château de Chillon; winter sports.

1815 Clarens - Montreux VD
Tel (021) 9644411
Fax (021) 9647002
Location overlooking lake;
ample car parking
Meals breakfast, lunch,
dinner, snacks
Prices rooms SS-SSSS with
breakfast
Rooms 5 double; 1 single; 1
suite; all have bath or shower,
central heating, phone, TV,
radio, minibar, hairdrier
Facilities dining-room;

terrace, garden
Credit cards AE, DC, MC, V
Children welcome
Disabled not suitable
Pets accepted
Closed Christmas and New
Year; restaurant only, Sun,
Mon
Languages English, French,
German
Proprietors Etienne and
Isabelle Krebs

Suisse Romande

Les Marines

'I surprised myself,' admitted our inspector, who happily reversed his unfavourable first impression after a tour. Totally modern, this hotel was designed to blend into the landscape; it succeeds. There are plenty of flowers and plants plus the best-kept lawn in Switzerland – on the roof. So well camouflaged is this two-storey building, you have to look carefully to spot it between the main road and the lake.

Inside, light filters on to marble floors through skylights in the lawn above, creating a peaceful atmosphere. As for bedrooms, 'these are large enough to play table-tennis in and that's without opening the terrace windows facing the lake'. Furnishings of light grey and pink are in 'hotel' style but, although they lack the personal touch, there is plenty of cupboard and shelf space. Our reporter, a family man, noted that each has a kitchenette which can be opened if required, and that the first-rate insulation means parents have no worries about noise. He reckoned this was a 'find' for anyone travelling on business or for a weekend away with children. The three dining-rooms are rather soulless, but there is a large terrace for outdoor dining.

Nearby Château de Chillon, public swimming-pool, water sports.

1844 Villeneuve, Montreux VD
Tel (021) 9603906
Fax (021) 9603934
E-mail suissemajestic@bluewin.ch
Location by the lake, just off route 9; ample car parking
Meals breakfast, lunch, dinner, snacks
Prices rooms SS-SSSS with breakfast
Rooms 21 double; 1 single; 2 suites; 1 family; all have bath or shower, central heating,
phone, TV, radio, minibar, hairdrier, safe
Facilities 3 dining-rooms, lift/elevator; terrace, garden
Credit cards AE, DC, MC, V
Children very welcome
Disabled reasonable access
Pets accepted
Closed end Oct to Easter
Languages English, French, German, Italian
Proprietors Gottdiener family

Suisse Romande

Hôtel Fleur du Lac

Rodolphe Schelbert is a true professional. Having started as a bell hop, he rose to manage a world-wide hotel chain; after retiring, he bought this property which he runs with more innovative ideas than we have seen in ten hotel groups put together. Although the building is not pretty, thousands of flowers at the entrance and in the garden soften the line. Inside, furnishings are old-fashioned but nicely so. All bedrooms face south, with splendid views over the lake to the distant Mont Blanc. Fabric covers walls, and bedspreads match curtains or chairs; bathrooms can be small but towels are big and fluffy. Like the trouser presses and special telephone/fax mach Fines, these were not available in Switzerland so M. Schelbert imports them himself.

Children are not just tolerated but catered for, with paper and pencils ready in the dining-room, where those on half-board are not relegated to a second-class menu but choose from the *menu du jour* or get a credit for à la carte dishes. Every guest gets a VIP. passport giving free entry to local museums, boat rides and even a free ice cream. 'Small enough to care' is the motto of Rudolphe and Elsbeth Schelbert's hotel. They do.

Nearby lake, Chillon, Morges castles, Pavillon Audrey Hepburn.

1110 Morges, route de Lausanne 70 VD
Tel (021) 8115811
Fax (021) 8115888
E-mail hotel@fleur-du-lac.ch
Location by lake; ample car parking **Meals** breakfast, lunch, dinner, snacks
Prices rooms SS-SSSS with breakfast
Rooms 25 double; 3 single; 2 suites; all have bath or shower, central heating, phone, TV, radio, minibar, hairdrier, safe, trouser press
Facilities dining-room, sitting-room, bar, sauna and fitness area, lift/elevator; 3 terraces, garden
Credit cards AE, DC, MC, V
Children very welcome
Disabled reasonable access to a few rooms **Pets** accepted
Closed never
Languages English, French, German, Italian, Dutch, Japanese, Portuguese
Proprietors Schelbert family

Suisse Romande

Le Vieux Manoir au Lac

'Looks more Norman than Swiss' was our inspector's first reaction to this lakeside manor house. He was right and even today, the French general from Normandy who built it a century ago would have little trouble finding his way around, despite the extensive and expensive renovations. Every room is full of the freshest flowers, old blends with new and even the corridors are notable, with high, decorated ceïlings. Bedrooms incorporate a sitting area and are furnished in 'exquisite taste', with fabric on the walls toning with sofa and chair coverings, often in bold patterns. Best of all are the two small, hexagonal suites in the old tower, with windows overlooking the park and lake, and light all day long, 'though it must take hours to draw all those curtains'.

The restaurant in the conservatory features the palest wood, with yellow and violet linen. 'Rather flowery for my taste' commented our reporter, who insisted that guests should come downstairs in the morning, rather than having breakfast in bed. 'You must see the breakfast-room with its natural wood floor in geometric design. Coloured glass on the chandeliers reflects the yellow ceiling and the bright red and green fabric on the walls.'
Nearby the medieval town of Murten.

3280 Murten-Meyriez FR
Tel (026) 6786161
Fax (026) 6786162
E-mail vieuxmanoir@bluewin.ch
Location rue de Lausanne on the lake; ample car parking
Meals breakfast, lunch, dinner, snacks
Prices rooms SSSS with breakfast
Rooms 28 double; 2 suites; all have bath or shower, central heating, phone, TV, radio, minibar, hairdrier

facilities 2 dining-rooms, sitting-room, lift/elevator; terrace, garden
Credit cards AE, DC, MC, V
Children welcome
Disabled not suitable
Pets accepted
Closed mid-Dec to mid-Feb
Languages English, French, German, Italian
Proprietors Elisabeth and Erich Thomas

Suisse Romande

La Maison du Prussien

At the heart of the Swiss watch-making region, Neuchâtel is an attractive city on the shore of Switzerland's largest lake. Home to language schools and educational institutions, the area is known for the clarity of its spoken French. For 150 years, however, the region was part of Prussia, which explains the name of the hotel, which readers have pressed us to include.

Out at the Gor du Vauseyon, a spectacular gorge with gushing waterfalls, this former brewery has been tastefully converted. The plain stone walls and exposed beams throughout retain the atmosphere of the 18thC building, while bedrooms are named for former owners, such as Suzanne Merveilleux and the brewer, Brasseur Andres. One of the most romantic is the Jean Chambrier room under the eaves, with its vast wooden ceiling, grand beams and working log fireplace. All the bathrooms are modern and luxurious; some have double tubs. Under the exacting management of Rolf and Francine Schneider, housekeeping is impeccable, while the restaurant, in an adjoining modern conservatory, has a growing reputation thanks to the cooking of young French chef, Jean-Yves Drevet.

Nearby the gorges, climbing wall; Neuchâtel and lake.

Au Gor du Vauseyon, 2006
Neuchâtel NE
Tel (032) 7305454
Fax (032) 7302143
Email maison-du-prussien@pointnet.ch
Location on edge of town; ample car parking
Meals breakfast, lunch, dinner, snacks
Prices rooms SS-SSS with breakfast
Rooms 10 double; all have bath or shower, central heating, telephone, TV, radio, hairdrier, VCR, minibar
Facilities sitting-room, 2 dining-rooms; terrace
Credit cards AE, DC, MC, V
Children very welcome
Disabled not suitable
Pets accepted
Closed never
Languages English, French, German, Italian
Managers Schneider family

Suisse Romande

Lakeside hotel, Coppet near Nyon

Hôtel du Lac

When the local 18thC Château was new, this hotel was already old. For 350 years it has offered hospitality to travellers. Arcades and façades present a decorative face to the Grande-Rue but the focus is the lake on the other side. Here you can swim, lie back on a sun lounger, or dine on the semi-circular curve of terrace, underneath an orange and white-striped awning. Bedrooms are large (you pay a premium for a view of the lake) but the suites are enormous. Our inspector was ready to move into one which even had a kitchen. The exposed joists of the attic ceiling are a dramatic feature, while the largest even has a private patio set into the slanting roof. He was less enthusiastic about the deep turquoise bathrooms.

With doors the thickness of an arm and heavy wooden furniture, the atmosphere is like a gentlemen's club, particularly in the plush smoking-room and large bar with its grand piano. 'Inviting armchairs, pity about the piped music,' was the reaction. In the restaurant, roasting is the order of the day, with the meat, poultry and fish turning on spits over the wood fire creating an almost medieval impression.

Nearby lake, Château de Coppet; golf, tennis, riding, sailing.

1296 Coppet VD
Tel (022) 7761521
Fax (022) 7765346
Location between main road and lake in Coppet; car parking on street, garage; private boat mooring
Meals breakfast, lunch, dinner, snacks
Prices rooms SS-SSSS; breakfast extra
Rooms 12 double; 7 suites; all have bath or shower, central heating, phone, TV, radio,
minibar
Facilities dining-room, 2 sitting-rooms, bar, lift/elevator; terrace, garden
Credit cards AE, DC, MC, V
Children welcome
Disabled not suitable
Pets accepted
Closed never
Languages English, French, German, Italian
Proprietors O. Schnyder

Suisse Romande

Village inn, Crans near Nyon

Auberge de Cerf

The owners have changed at this traditional inn in the heart of the vineyards which produce the La Côte wines. The popular Haroutunian family have moved on, replaced in 1997 by Roland and Laurence Petit. Already readers have commended this couple, who had been in the restaurant business for two decades on the shores of Lake Léman. Not surprisingly, their restaurant is still the main focus of attention, featuring fish from the nearby lake as well as free-range chickens from local farms. Their bistro is just as popular, with well-priced dishes for families and also for those wanting a quick, light meal.

Little has changed when it comes to decoration, however, so regulars with find reminders of Sandro Haroutunian. The antique furniture that he bought at auctions all over the country still add character to the plain bedrooms. These are not large, but every bit of space has been used, resulting in ceilings with strange angles, and some of the private bathrooms across the corridor, rather than en suite. Showers prevail; only the suite has a bath, but there are fresh flowers in the rooms. 'Very pink' is the brief description of the colour schemes.

Nearby lake, Richard Burton's grave; Nyon, Geneva.(20km)

1299 Crans-près-Nyon VD
Tel (022) 7762323
Fax (022) 7760221
Location in middle of village; reserved car parking nearby
Meals breakfast, lunch, dinner, snacks
Prices rooms SF80-160; breakfast SF10; DB&B from SF133; reduction for children; meals from SF43
Rooms 7 double; 2 single; all have bath or shower, central heating, phone, TV, radio
Facilities dining-room, sitting-room; garden
Credit cards AE, MC, V
Children very welcome
Disabled 2 special ground floor rooms planned for 1994
Pets accepted
Closed never; restaurant only, Sun eve, Mon
Languages English, French, German
Proprietors Haroutunian family

Suisse Romande

L'Ermitage

Bernard Ravet was Switzerland's chef of the year in 1993 and 1996 yet he remains a modest man. In 1989 he and his wife, Ruth, settled in this little village dominated by a huge château set in the midst of vineyards. Much of the 17thC farmhouse remains: brick floors lead to a bar and sitting-room with a huge 18thC fireplace and blue painted-wood ceiling. There is even a cat for appropriate laps. Of the 30,000 bottles in the wine cellar, much is local or from the New World for, despite his roots in Burgundy, M. Ravet delights in suggesting that his guests try something new.

A perfectionist, he insists on baking his bread in a wood-fired oven and smoking his own salmon and rabbit. Dishes range from a *gratin* of leeks, truffles and sweetbreads through lobster lasagna to exquisite desserts including kirsch soufflé served with cherry compote. A small room designed for summer dining joins the main building to the extension, whose six rooms and three suites look over the garden and are decorated with split cane furniture and large, old armoires. Our reporter gave an accolade to the bathrooms for the baths, generous showers, twin wash-basins, separate lavatory and towels as big as football fields.

Nearby Château, vineyards; Morges.

1134 Vufflens-le-Château, Morges VD
Tel (021) 8046868
Fax (021) 8022240
Location in village, near church
Meals breakfast, lunch, dinner, snacks
Prices rooms SSS-SSSS with breakfast
Rooms 6 double; 3 suites; all have bath or shower, central heating, phone, TV, radio, minibar, hairdrier

Facilities dining-room, sitting-room, bar, lift/elevator; terrace, garden
Credit cards AE, DC, MC, V
Children welcome
Disabled reasonable access
Pets accepted
Closed 3 weeks in Aug; 3 weeks in Dec; restaurant only, Sun, Mon
Languages English, French, German, Spanish
Proprietors Bernard and Ruth Ravet

Bern

Bären

Wherever our inspector went in the Berner Oberland, hoteliers mentioned the Bären in Adelboden. Innkeeper Peter Willen is a lifelong native of the village but it was only in 1989 that he bought this building, which dates back to 1500. Completely renovated, the inn now exudes a solid comfort and charm which fights shy of luxury and goes one up on *gemütlich*. Bedrooms have been named after the peaks in view and each has a different ambience. The Fitzer, a corner room, overlooks the park and the main street. Sniff the scent of new pine and admire the romantic, white-curtained, four-poster bed; stretch out – and it is a special airbed! The Grosslohner, on the other hand, is for families, with a spacious mezzanine area for the children under the extra-high ceiling.

The inevitable *Rösti*, served up in a cast iron skillet, is the pride of Peter Willen's Speisesaal, where *raclette* and fondues are also on offer. In the à la carte restaurant, the menu encompasses a full range of French and German dishes. Busy in winter and summer, Adelboden attracts many Dutch and Belgians, especially families. Do not look for the jet set here.

Nearby walking; winter sports.

3715 Adelboden BE
Tel (033) 6732151
Fax (033) 6732190
E-mail hotelbaeren@bluewin.ch
Location in middle of resort next to public park; underground car parking
Meals breakfast, lunch, dinner, snacks
Prices rooms S-SSS with breakfast
Rooms 11 double; 3 single; all have bath or shower, central heating, phone, TV, radio, minibar, hairdrier
Facilities 3 dining-rooms, bar, sauna, lift/elevator; terrace
Credit cards AE, DC, MC, V
Children welcome
Disabled limited access
Pets accepted
Closed end Nov to mid-Dec; mid-May to mid-Jun
Languages English, French, German, Italian
Proprietors Willen family

Bern

Fiescherblick

Grindelwald, the only one of the Jungfrau region's resorts that is accessible by car, is a paradise for sporty mountain lovers, who provide a loyal clientele for the Fiescherblick. Backpacks are piled in the doorway at 6 am or earlier, as ski tourers in winter and hikers in summer get ready to set off. The hotel knows all the local mountain guides, which trails to take, and even where to photograph the elusive edelweiss and gentian flowers.

Comfort rather than luxury typifies this inn, a modern version of the traditional Swiss mountain style. Some of the downstairs rooms have been renovated recently, using a combination of pale wood, white walls and mauve carpets and curtains. Others are still brown and white. That difference in furnishings also applies to bedrooms, and the 12 in the the new wing also have TV, phone and hairdriers. The older bedrooms, however, are perfectly acceptable: generously-sized and with up to date bathrooms. Everyone, however, can enjoy the food; not only does it look pretty on the plate, second helpings are always offered to half-board guests. Packed lunches and an early morning thermos of hot tea are all part of the service, which impressed our inspector.

Nearby Firstbahn; winter sports.

3818 Grindelwald BE
Tel (033) 8534453
Fax (033) 8534457
E-mail hotel@fiescherblick.ch
Location at far end of village from train station; ample car parking
Meals breakfast, lunch, dinner, snacks
Prices rooms S-SSS with breakfast
Rooms 25 double; all have bath or shower, central heating, minibar, safe; some

phone, TV, hairdrier
Facilities dining-room, sitting-room, bar, lift/elevator; terrace
Credit cards AE, DC, MC, V
Children welcome
Disabled not suitable
Pets accepted
Closed 20 Nov to 20 Dec; after Easter to 20 May
Languages English, French, German, Italian
Proprietor 'Johnny' Brawand

Bern

❈ Village inn, Grosshöchstetten ❈

Sternen

From the outside, this *Landgasthof* looks like many others we have seen. A former farmhouse, dating from the 18thC, it became a restaurant a century ago and has the decorative paintwork and colourful shutters that we expect of Swiss country inns. Only 25 km away from Bern, it is a favourite destination of diplomats who want to show their guests a typical rural pub. No wonder the visitors' book boasts signatures such as HRH Prince Philip and President Jimmy Carter.

The Stettler family have been hosts at the Sternen for two generations but have been hotel-keepers for 125 years. One of their specialities is the local ham, cured in Grandfather's chimney and highly-rated by our inspector. 'I don't know what he puts on the fire, but the delicious flavour will stay with me for a long time.' Hearty appetites are appreciated and catered for, with guests on half-board offered 'double helpings'. Afterwards, calories may be worked off in the *Kegelbahnen* (bowling alleys) Overall, the look is traditional and rather simple, though there is a hand-painted ceiling in the panelled dining-room. Upstairs, bedrooms have peasant-style wardrobes and small bathrooms.

Nearby Bern; tennis, swimming, walking; winter sports.

3506 Grosshöchstetten BE
Tel (031) 7102424
Fax (031) 7102425
Location in middle of village; own car parking
Meals breakfast, lunch, dinner, snacks
Prices rooms S-SS with breakfast
Rooms 6 double; 2 single; 2 family; all have bath or shower, central heating, phone; some TV
Facilities 2 dining-rooms, bowling alleys; terrace
Credit cards MC, V
Children welcome
Disabled not suitable
Pets accepted
Closed never; restaurant only, Mon
Languages English, French, German
Proprietor Jürg Stettler

Bern

❊ Town inn, Gstaad ❊

Hotel Olden

Swiss hotel-keeping may be world-famous but it is the individual hoteliers who become legends. Heidi Donizetti was as big a star as her regular guests, who included Roger Moore, Robert Wagner and Julie Andrews. Today, despite new owners, a new manager and welcome renovations, our readers report that the Olden is still their favourite spot in this high-powered resort.

The chalet-style inn, brightened by green shutters and the usual window boxes of red geraniums, is also still frequented by the local farmers who stop in for a drink, pretending to be oblivious to the jet setters who come to dine and dance.

The food, which is 'as good as ever', includes local specialities as well as international dishes. Among the recent improvements are a cosy bar with a fireplace and a terrace. The few bedrooms retain their individuality, as well as some of the cupboards and doors painted by Heidi over the years. Although right on the busy main road, the majority are in an annexe at the back, separated by an upstairs terrace for private sunbathing. The very large, very quiet garden is the only green lawn to be seen in downtown Gstaad.

Nearby walking, swimming; winter sports.

3780 Gstaad BE
Tel (033) 744 3444
Fax (033) 744 6164
Location in middle of town; car parking nearby
Meals breakfast, lunch, dinner, snacks
Prices rooms SSS-SSSS with breakfast
Rooms 11 double; 4 single; all have bath or shower, central heating, phone, TV, radio, minibar; some hairdrier
Facilities 2 dining-rooms, sitting-room, bar; terrace, garden
Credit cards AE, DC, MC, V
Children welcome
Disabled not suitable
Pets accepted
Closed mid-Apr to mid-May
Languages English, French, German, Italian, Spanish
Manager Gianni Biggi

Bern

❊ Golf hotel, Gstaad at Saanenmöser ❊

Les Hauts de Gstaad

The hotel has a reputation for entertaining the *beau monde* during Gstaad's 'social' season. Any formality implied by the elegant fabrics and designer colours in the entrance is quickly shattered, thanks to the relaxed professionalism of the staff.

Although modernised completely in 1985, the building is full of antiques, such as the museum-quality Bernese Oberland baby carriages. In daily use, however, is the 26-passenger 1949 yellow post bus. As for food, guests choose the dining-room according to their mood: the Belle Epoque for classic French, the Winter-Garten for half-board guests, and the Bärengraben for Swiss specialities such as *raclette* and fondue in informal surroundings complete with murals of bears. The Dolce Vita, of course, is strictly Italian.

Bedrooms, mostly of the same size and design, have hand-carved pine doors, painted wooden beds and large, white-tiled bathrooms with double wash-basins. Although next to a working farm, there is nothing rustic here; this is a retreat for city folk who enjoy sports, particularly ski-ing and the new 18-hole golf course.

Nearby golf, mountain biking, walking; winter sports.

3777 Saanenmöser-Gstaad BE
Tel (033) 7486868
Fax (033) 7486800
Location above Saanenmöser; car parking, some covered
Meals breakfast, lunch, dinner, snacks
Prices rooms SS-SSSS with breakfast
Rooms 24 double; 6 single; all have bath or shower, central heating, phone, TV, radio, minibar, hairdrier, safe
Facilities 4 dining-rooms, sitting-room, bar, sauna, fitness area, lift/elevator; terrace, garden, 2 tennis courts
Credit cards AE, DC, MC, V
Children welcome
Disabled not suitable
Pets accepted
Closed mid-Oct to mid-Dec; Easter to end Apr
Languages English, French, German, Italian, Spanish
Proprietor Franz Wehren
Manager Siebenthal family

Bern

Hirschen

A former owner of this inn was jailed for selling liquor, but the hostelry now has a licence – the permit was granted back in 1666. Peter and Marianne Graf-Sterchi are the ninth successive generation to run this hostelry, originally a farmhouse and dating from the 1500s.

Hospitality must run in their blood for nowhere did we receive a warmer welcome, and that was on a busy night with all the rooms full. Not content with hotel-keeping, they have a farm up in Wengen where they raise black Angus cattle and also gardens in Wilderswil producing salads, herbs and vegetables. They even keep their own chickens and geese.

Although the hotel has been renovated, new wood blends with ancient timbers as antiques do with modern, but traditionally-styled furniture. Bedrooms vary in size but all are comfortable and pleasantly decorated, even if they would not win any design awards. Who cares, when breakfast can be taken on the balcony with the Jungfrau standing out against deep blue sky? We would be happy to settle in and forget the crowds of tourists in nearby Interlaken.

Nearby riding, tennis, walking; winter sports.

3800 Interlaken-Matten BE
Tel (033) 8221545
Fax (033) 8233745
Location on north side of Interlaken; ample car parking
Meals breakfast, lunch, dinner, snacks
Prices rooms S-SSS with breakfast
Rooms 17 double; 5 single; all have bath or shower, central heating, phone, radio, TV
Facilities 2 dining-rooms, sitting-room, bar, sauna, fitness area; terrace, garden
Credit cards AE, DC, MC, V
Children very welcome
Disabled not suitable
Pets accepted
Closed Nov; restaurant only, Tues
Languages English, French, German
Proprietors Peter and Marianne Graf-Sterchi

Bern

❋ **Mountain chalet, Kandersteg** ❋

Ruedihus

'Never have I seen a better-preserved example of authentic Oberland style and atmosphere,' our inspector wrote wistfully, wishing he could stay longer. The setting is 'cinematic': open pastures ringed on three sides by mountains. Sitting in the flower garden, under maple trees, 'I hear only the occasional moo of a grazing cow'. Waxing poetic, he described the hand-carved patterns on the sun-seared exterior, enlivened by various types of wood and leaded window panes. Although renovated in 1990 to put in modern heating and plumbing, this 18thC house still looks like a museum of traditional life. There are *Kachelöfen* and hand-painted chests plus a rocking horse, a children's size farm wagon and an embroidery frame, with fabric ready to stitch. The high, open rafters and generous four-poster bed make the Rosserstübli a favourite, but the Grosserstübli also has a four-poster, hung with floral fabrics. 'Grandma's' jam, home-made from mountain berries, appears on the breakfast table and may be bought by the jar. The Maeder family use only Swiss-made products; there is, therefore, no Coca-Cola. Credit cards are an unacceptable intrusion of the modern world. Cash only, please.
Nearby walking, para-gliding; winter sports.

3718 Kandersteg BE
Tel (033) 6758182
Fax (033) 6758158
Location in meadows below mountains; ample car parking
Meals breakfast, lunch, dinner, snacks
Prices rooms S-SSS with breakfast
Rooms 8 double; 1 single; all have bath or shower, central heating, phone, radio, hairdrier
Facilities 4 dining-rooms, sitting-room; terrace, garden
Credit cards not accepted
Children very welcome
Disabled not suitable
Pets accepted
Closed never
Languages English, French, German, Italian
Proprietors Maeder family

Bern

Doldenhorn

This is a hotel where regulars settle in and stay, often for three or four weeks in the summer. They stretch out and read on *chaise-longues* in the garden, play chess on the giant outdoor board, fish in the tree-shaded trout stream and stroll in the three acres of grounds. Children enjoy the swings, the sandpit and feeding the ducks on the pond. Some savour the seclusion and beauty of the dramatic granite cliff that rears up behind the hotel; others head off hiking and para-gliding.

The Maeder family, who also own the nearby Ruedihus, have been here for 50 years, and their inn is an intriguing blend of old and new. In the lobby, the first thing you see is an antique but working telephone, made in Stockholm and nearly as big as a telecommunications satellite. An even bigger cowbell summons the receptionist. Bedroom keys, however, are electronic. In the Gourmet restaurant, starched white linen and striped silk chair upholstery create a formal look while the opposite effect is achieved in the *Burestube* by oval pine tables, hanging lamps and unfinished plank floors. Each bedroom is different; many have paintings of local mountain scenes. Bathrooms are functional.
Nearby para-gliding, walking; winter sports.

3718 Kandersteg BE
Tel (033) 6758181
Fax (033) 6758185
Location in woods outside village; ample car parking
Meals breakfast, lunch, dinner, snacks
Prices rooms S-SSS with breakfast
Rooms 26 double; 3 single; all have bath or shower, central heating, phone, TV, radio, minibar, hairdrier
Facilities 3 dining-rooms,

2 sitting-rooms, sauna, lift/elevator; terrace, garden
Credit cards AE, DC, MC, V
Children very welcome
Disabled not suitable
Pets accepted
Closed Nov
Languages English, French, German
Proprietors Maeder family

Bern

Lakeside hotel, Ligerz

Kreuz

Ligerz boasts a museum of wine and over three-quarters of the small population works in the surrounding vineyards. Not to be outdone, the Hotel Kreuz has its own vines producing its own wine and even its own *marc*. This inn dates back to 1345, has been in the same family for 200 years but is still full of surprises, thanks to the enterprise of the present owners who worked in Canada and Australia before coming home to take over the business. 'My father-in-law just milked the cow,' explains Kaspar Mettler-Teutsch as he reels off the work done and his plans for the future. Recent additions include Le Jardin, a lakeside bistro, and a new steam bath and sauna. Bedrooms have a mixture of antique and very modern furniture; 'I liked my quirky old chair,' wrote our inspector, who reckoned the large towels and excellent showers would satisfy any North American. Windows look over Lake Biel, and although the view is interrupted by the local road and a single track railway line, neither is intrusive.

Downstairs, it seems the whole village is either eating or drinking in the restaurant but hotel guests are welcomed as honorary locals.

Nearby vineyards; water sports.

2514 Ligerz BE
Tel (032) 3151115
Fax (032) 3152814
Location on lake; limited car parking in front of hotel
Meals breakfast, lunch, dinner, snacks
Prices rooms S-SS with breakfast
Rooms 16 double; all have bath or shower, central heating, phone, TV
Facilities dining-room, bar, sauna, lift/elevator; terrace, garden
Credit cards AE, DC, MC, V
Children very welcome
Disabled good access; 1 room specially designed
Pets not accepted
Closed 3 weeks in Jan; restaurant only, Wed
Languages English, French, German, Italian, Portuguese
Proprietors Kaspar and Liselotte Mettler-Teutsch

Bern

❋ Mountain inn, Brünig Pass ❋

Brünig Kulm

Perched half-way up the Brünig Pass, this looks like a typical Bernese Oberland chalet that has been here for centuries, though it is only 17 years old. At a height of some 1,000 m, the view is, when the cloud allows, pure picture-postcard. Open the bedroom window, lean on the sill and watch the water spray from seven waterfalls into the valley opposite, famous for the town of Meiringen (and therefore for meringues) and for the case of the disappearing detective. It was in 'that bottomless abyss' of the Reichenbach falls that Sherlock Holmes and Professor Moriarty tumbled to their deaths – or did they?

Although the pass is not that high and Brünig is no more than a hamlet, with only four or five houses, this is popular with skiers in winter and walkers in summer who appreciate the simple pleasures. Their hearty appetites do justice to Herr Schweizer's specialities such as *raclette* and 'three fillets'. The latter consists of three separate plates, each with a different grilled meat and accompanying vegetables or pasta: just like eating three main courses in succession. Bedrooms are panelled in wood and plainly furnished, with curtains made from locally-woven fabric.

Nearby Sherlock Holmes Museum, walking; winter sports.

6082 Brünig BE
Tel (033) 9711708
Fax (033) 9711749
Location half-way up Brünig Pass; ample car parking
Meals breakfast, lunch, dinner, snacks
Prices rooms S-SS with breakfast
Rooms 8 double; most have bath or shower, central heating, phone, minibar
Facilities 3 dining-rooms; terrace

Credit cards AE, DC, MC, V
Children very welcome
Disabled not suitable
Pets accepted
Closed 3 weeks Jan; restaurant only, Wed; Thurs in winter
Languages English, French, German, Italian, Danish
Proprietors Schweizer family

Bern

❊ **Mountain inn, near Schangnau im Emmental** ❊

Kemmeriboden-Bad

'Don't worry about finding this hotel; if you turn off at Schangnau, just follow the beautiful valley as it narrows, and the road ends in the car park.' When it was built over 150 years ago, the sulphur springs provided the attraction here. They still do, but now visitors also come for the canoeing, fishing, walking, and mountain-climbing in summer, and the skiing in winter. Summer weekends can be busy, with local families driving out for specialities such as meringues, but somehow it never feels overcrowded. 'Perhaps that's because there is so much for children to do' decided our inspector, who noted the table-tennis and play ground.

Although recently modernised, the original house contains large, traditional bedrooms, many with antique furniture but modern beds. In the extension, some bedrooms can sleep up to six, with a double bed and two sets of bunks. The balconies are useful for drying boots and jackets. Our man wondered if the 'ghastly' brown tiles in the bathrooms were chosen because of the inevitable mud from outdoor pursuits. There are also separate, simpler rooms without private bathrooms for groups.

Nearby sulphur springs; hiking, swimming; winter sports.

6197 Schangnau im Emmental BE
Tel (034) 4937777
Fax (034) 4937770
Location in meadows; ample car parking
Meals breakfast, lunch, dinner, snacks
Prices rooms S-SS with breakfast
Rooms 21 double; 8 single; all have bath or shower, central heating, phone, TV, radio, minibar; additional simpler rooms
Facilities 2 dining-rooms, sitting-room, lift/elevator; terrace, garden
Credit cards AE, DC, MC, V
Children very welcome
Disabled accessible via lift/elevator **Pets** accepted
Closed Dec; restaurant only, Mon; Tues (Jan to May)
Languages English, French, German, Italian
Proprietors Invernizzi-Gerber family

Bern

Strandhotel Belvédère

Many consider the Bay of Spiez to be one of the most beautiful in Europe, with the 11thC tower of a château, 12thC church and white sailboats on the water. Markus Schneider agrees and likes nothing better than to sit in the hotel's flower-filled garden, sipping a chilled Riesling-Sylvaner vintage from the vineyards within view just across the bay. Along with fellow manager Rosmarie Seiler-Bigler, he supervises weekly 'grill parties'. Our reporter reckons these must be better than the average barbecue because the Swiss Butcher's Association has its school next door. The association also owns the hotel and paid for a total overhaul in 1992.

The restaurants at Strandhotel Belvédère serve fish from the lake and light, easy-to-digest dishes. The Blue Room, used for breakfast, is very grand with high ceilings, twin grandfather clocks and blue velvet floor-to-ceiling curtains. Inlaid woods, silks and antique curiosities throughout create a refined atmosphere. Bedroom decoration follows subtle flower themes. In number 206, for example, light from three bay windows floods on to a pretty rose-patterned bedspread.

Nearby water sports, own beach.

3700 Spiez BE **Tel** (033) 6543333 **Fax** (033) 6546633 **Location** in large park on shore of lake; ample car parking **Meals** breakfast, lunch, dinner, snacks **Prices** rooms SS-SSSS with breakfast **Rooms** 30 double; 3 single; all have bath or shower, central heating, phone, TV, radio, minibar, hairdrier	**Facilities** 3 dining-rooms, 3 sitting-rooms, lift/elevator; terrace, garden, private beach **Credit cards** AE, DC, MC, V **Children** welcome **Disabled** not suitable **Pets** accepted **Closed** Oct to Mar **Languages** English, French, German, Italian **Managers** Rosmarie Seiler-Bigler and Markus Schneider

Bern

❋ Wayside inn, Trubschachen ❋

Hirschen

Here in the Emmental, hospitality and cuisine come naturally, so after a day walking in the valley, visiting farms and watching the famous cheese mature, there can be nothing better than retiring, hungry, to a nearby inn and asking for the local speciality. This is the *Berner Platte*, a challenge to the heartiest appetites. 'I did my best, but couldn't finish the mountain of meat and sausages surrounded by sauerkraut and boiled potatoes,' admitted our inspector, who had never felt so full in his life but was ready to breakfast on delicious Emmental cheese next morning.

'The food is as typically Bernese as the rest of this hostelry; I could even hear jolly singing in the bar.' The family has been here since 1872 and nowadays a host of relatives help with the running of this unpretentious hotel. The Rôtisserie, with its rough ceiling-beams and stone wall has more character than other rooms. 'Modern rustic' is the overall look, with lots of wood but no fancy frills; bedrooms, for example, are straightforward, with small, basic bathrooms. Prices are inexpensive for this country, so this is just the place for families, sporty types and anyone travelling on a budget.

Nearby mountain biking, walking; winter sports.

3555 Trubschachen im Emmental BE
Tel (034) 4955115
Fax (034) 4955552
Location at roadside in village; own car parking
Meals breakfast, lunch, dinner, snacks
Prices rooms S with breakfast
Rooms 4 double; 2 single; all have bath or shower, central heating, phone
Facilities 3 dining-rooms, sitting-room; terrace

Credit cards AE, MC, V
Children very welcome
Disabled not suitable
Pets accepted
Closed 3 weeks Jan; last week July; first week Aug; restaurant only, Mon, Tues lunch
Languages English, French, German, Italian
Proprietors Soltermann-Brunner family

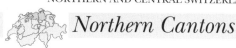

Northern Cantons

Art hotel, Basel

Teufelhof

After years of experience in the theatre, Monica and Dominique Thommy decided to unite their love of the stage and culture with their love of gastronomy. The result, a mini arts complex, opened in 1989. 'We hope people coming to the theatre will try the cooking of chef Michael Baader in the restaurants; we want the gourmets to look at the bedrooms with their "environment-art"; and we encourage hotel guests to visit the theatre.' It may sound complicated but it works, according to our inspector who pronounced this inn 'unique'.

'Yes, there are other hotels in Switzerland that look like art galleries, with superb collections of paintings, but here the eight bedrooms themselves are works of art.' Each was created, not just decorated, by a different artist. The only condition was to maintain a high standard of comfort. As is always the case with art, 'you may like some and loathe others' warned our reporter. In any case, the bedrooms will be gutted after two years, leaving the canvas blank for another artist's imagination.

Like our man, you may not understand all the jokes in the cabaret but you will enjoy this theatrical experience.
Nearby old town and its attractions.

4051 Basel, Leonhardsgraben 47/Heuberg 30 BS
Tel (061) 2611010
Fax (061) 2611004
Location in heart of old town; public car parking nearby
Meals breakfast, lunch, dinner, snacks
Prices rooms SS-SSSS with breakfast
Rooms 33 double; all have bath or shower, central heating, phone, hairdrier, works of art

Facilities 3 dining-rooms, bar; terrace
Credit cards AE, DC, MC, V
Children welcome
Disabled not suitable
Pets accepted
Closed Christmas to mid-Jan; restaurant only, Sun, Mon
Languages English, French, German, Italian
Proprietors Monica and Dominique Thommy

Northern Cantons

Zum Ochsen

One must never discount suburbia when looking for well-run hotels. Take the number 10 tram out of Basel and after a 15-minute ride you are in Arlesheim, where streets in the old part of town are still cobbled. Just outside are vineyards, with a small old château looming above. Many people stay at the Ochsen when attending the nearby homeopathic hospital or going to the huge theatre at Dornach for productions of Shakespeare and Goethe, whose *Faust* plays here at its full length over ten days.

'I'd be happy to stay here' commented our reporter, who liked this inn, founded in 1692 by a family of butchers whose descendants help to run the restaurant. 'Not for vegetarians though' he warned, since gilded bulls heads, model pigs and cartoons of every sort of animal adorn the walls, while the speciality is calves' liver with a perfect *Rösti*. The oak panelling here was saved during the 1990 rebuilding but elsewhere, walls are of cool marble. Bedrooms are simple: pale colours and furniture in wild pear wood are offset by antiques and paintings by a local artist. Those on upper floors look out on the cathedral or nearby hills and vineyards.

Nearby Basel, Dornach with theatre.

4144 Arlesheim, Eremitagestr 16 BL
Tel (061) 7065200
Fax (061) 7065254
Location near Dorfplatz; car parking in own garage
Meals breakfast, lunch, dinner, snacks
Prices rooms S-SS with breakfast
Rooms 15 double; 20 single; all have bath or shower, central heating, phone, TV, radio, minibar; no smoking floor
Facilities 2 dining-rooms, sitting-room, conservatory, lift/elevator
Credit cards AE, DC, MC, V
Children welcome
Disabled not suitable
Pets accepted
Closed never
Languages English, French, German, Italian, Portuguese
Proprietors Daniel Jenzer and Max Schmid

Northern Cantons

Restaurant with rooms, Kaiseraugst

Landgasthof Adler

'A typical *Landgasthof*, the heart of village social life' was the description of this inn, full of old world charm and hospitality. Our readers agree, and endorse the new management team who maintain the efficient service. Swap the outdoor key for your bedroom key in the electronic dispenser and let yourself in to a brand-new bedroom boasting a telephone line designated for your personal computer. Just because this inn was built in the 17thC, don't expect anything less than the latest in 20thC facilities.

Some bedrooms have a cabin feeling, with wood furniture and panelling; those up in the eaves offer more room to manoeuvre. Furnishings are straightforward and simple; bathrooms are tiny, with only a shower, but bright and clean. Although the restaurant has been modernised, the original Gaststube still has its ceramic wood-burning stove and is full of gossiping locals. The owners' pride and joy is the wine cellar, with bottles from Switzerland, France, and even California. There are no stairs down, just a lift/elevator which our inspector reckoned was adapted from a fork lift truck. Once again, the 20thC coming to the aid of the 17th. **Nearby** ferry stop for Basel; cycling, hiking.

4303 Kaiseraugst, Dorfstr 35 AG
Tel (061) 8111111
Fax (061) 8113894
Location in middle of village; own car parking
Meals breakfast, lunch, dinner, snacks
Prices rooms SF95-160 with breakfast; reduction for children; meals from SF15
Rooms 7 double; 4 single; all have bath or shower, central heating, phone, radio, minibar; TV on request
Facilities 2 dining-rooms, sitting-room; terrace
Credit cards AE, DC, MC, V
Children welcome
Disabled not suitable
Pets accepted
Closed late Aug to mid-Sept; restaurant only, Wed, Thurs
Languages English, French, German, Italian
Proprietors Christian and Gaby Jung

Northern Cantons

City hotel, Zurich

Tiefenau

Imagine visiting a maiden aunt whose 160-year-old house is on a tree-lined street just five minutes' walk from the University. Inside, patterned carpets on marble floors, potted plants on window sills and lots of inviting chairs and sofas add up to a look that is genteel and comfortable, rather than grand. Just as in a private home, rooms are not 'designed' but are full of antiques that look as if they have been collected over the years. Even the cigarettes are not in a vending machine but in an old glass case next to a basket of healthier apples for guests to pick up and crunch. Actors and musicians are among the regular clientele who relax over drinks in the bar and in the small, airy library stocked with books in several languages.

Every bedroom is completely different, perhaps with split cane furniture and winged-armchairs, though as in many conversions of old houses, bathrooms end up being rather small. The compensation is that they have every modern luxury, with marble basins, cosmetic bars and even weighing scales for the health-conscious. The restaurant specialises in local Zurich dishes, and, in summer, there is dining in the garden.

Nearby University, Museum of Fine Art, theatre.

8032 Zurich, Steinwiesstr 8-10 ZH
Tel (01) 2678787
Fax (01) 2512476
E-mail info@tiefenau.ch
Location near middle of city, on east bank; own car parking, garage nearby
Meals breakfast, lunch, dinner, snacks
Prices rooms SF170-350 with breakfast; reduction for children; meals from SF25
Rooms 10 double; 3 single; 5 suites; all have bath or shower, central heating, phone, TV, radio, minibar, hairdrier, safe, e-mail access
Facilities 2 dining-rooms, sitting-room, bar, lift/elevator; terrace **Credit cards** AE, DC, MC, V **Children** welcome
Disabled access to 1 bedroom
Pets accepted **Closed** Christmas and New Year
Languages English, French, German, Italian, Spanish
Proprietor Beat Blumer

Northern Cantons

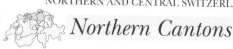

Ermitage

'An oasis of peace and tranquillity' was our inspector's immediate reaction as he turned off the main coast road and drove into the secluded grounds with their scented gardens.

The banks and businesses of Zurich are just a seven-minute drive away but the atmosphere here is of a holiday resort. Sail and motorboats are moored just off the shore, where tables and a huge circular bar are shaded by cheerful yellow and white umbrellas. There is even a beach club. Add in the outstanding restaurant with its '*Cuisine Niçoise*', described as 'French cuisine with a breeze of Italy' and it is easy to see why this is a favourite with executives, particularly the younger set.

The 300-year-old house was converted to a hotel some 40 years ago, but the inside is 'just what you would expect of a small, exclusive retreat in the 1990s'. That means plush furnishings in subtle colours, original art on the walls, antiques and fresh flowers in every room. The large reception area feels like a spacious sitting-room. Beds are enormous, as are the white-marble bathrooms with vast towels, but readers warn that rooms at the back are disappointingly cramped.

Nearby lake, Zurich.

8700 Küsnacht-Zurich, Seestr 80 ZH
Tel (01) 9144242
Fax (01) 9144243
E-mail info@ermitage.ch
Location off main lakeside road, on shore; own car parking
Meals breakfast, lunch, dinner, snacks
Prices rooms SS-SSSS with breakfast
Rooms 16 double; 4 single; 6 suites; all have bath or shower, central heating, phone, TV, radio, minibar, hairdrier, safe
Facilities 2 dining-rooms, sitting-room, bar, lift/elevator; terrace, garden
Credit cards AE, DC, MC, V
Children welcome
Disabled not suitable
Pets accepted
Closed never
Languages English, French, German, Italian
Manager Martin Hintermann

Northern Cantons

Suburban hotel, Zurich at Rüschlikon

Belvoir

This purpose-built hotel, dating from 1978, caters mainly to business travellers and conference guests. From the driveway, only the roof of the top storey is visible; the other two are set into the hillside. This slopes down towards the distant shore of Lake Zurich, which stretches away to the right and left as if seen through a wide-angled camera lens. Outside, gardens, statues and fountains soften the modern lines of the building, while inside, furnishings are more 'city' than 'country', particularly in the bar with its stylish polished marble and granite. There are three restaurants, ranging from the formal to the casual and these host special events; our inspector arrived during 'Chinese week', for example. This sort of variety is part of the careful planning that impressed our man, who noted that the conference hall occasionally stages musical evenings. If you don't feel like culture, then retire to the two traditional bowling alleys in the lower level. Bedrooms are decorated in low-key colours and although quite large, our reporter advises paying just a bit more to upgrade to the spacious junior suites. Staff are very hospitable; 'none of your paid-for smiles here'.

Nearby Zurich, lake.

8803 Rüschlikon-Zurich,
Säumerstr 37 ZH
Tel (01) 7046464
Fax (01) 7046465
E-mail info@belvoirhotel.ch
Location on hillside, overlooking lake; own car parking, some covered
Meals breakfast, lunch, dinner, snacks
Prices rooms SSS-SSSS with breakfast; reduction for children; meals from SF45
Rooms 25 double; 1 suite; all have bath or shower, central heating, phone, TV, radio, minibar
Facilities 3 dining-rooms, bar, lift/elevator; terrace, garden
Credit cards AE, DC, MC, V
Children welcome
Disabled good access
Pets accepted
Closed never
Languages English, French, German, Italian
Proprietor Peter Hugi

Central Cantons

Restaurant with rooms, Altendorf

Hecht

Why is the the canton of Schwyz, the cradle of the Swiss nation, so popular with business people? A low tax rate, of course, which has revived the fortunes of this area, perhaps for the first time in the 400 years since the local Bishop decided to move across the lake from Altendorf to Rapperswil. The Hecht has been the local inn since the 15thC, but some 20 years ago the restaurant business began to expand, so the concrete-block extension was added.

Now the quality of the cooking, especially fish dishes, attracts people from all around Lake Zurich. Some arrive by boat and sit out on the waterside terrace under cream sunshades. The vista is the same inside the formal restaurant; here furnishings are boldly contemporary, with deep rose-coloured table-cloths standing out against the blues and grays of carpet and curtains. A traditional feel remains, however, in the Hechtstübli, the informal restaurant which serves light meals.

The bedrooms are also in the old part of the house, dating from the 17thC and with the creaky floors to prove it. Simply decorated, with wood-panelled walls and painted furniture, they have small, basic bathrooms.

Nearby Lake Zurich.

8852 Altendorf SZ
Tel (055) 4510100
Fax (055) 4510101
Location on lake shore; ample car parking
Meals breakfast, lunch, dinner, snacks
Prices rooms SS-SSS with breakfast
Rooms 6 double; 1 suite; all have bath or shower, phone, TV, radio, minibar
Facilities 2 dining-rooms; terrace, garden

Credit cards AE, DC, MC, V
Children very welcome
Disabled not suitable
Pets accepted
Closed 2 weeks Jan
Languages English, French, German, Italian
Proprietor Hansjörg Jenny

Central Cantons

Old coaching inn, Amsteg

Stern und Post

Goethe, the great German poet, was a guest here. Although he argued over the prices with the hotelier, today's guests are usually more than satisfied, even though changes have been made since Elisabeth Tresch took over from her late brother. Her slight American accent was acquired at Cornell University, NY, but her family have been here since 1474 and she has a wealth of knowledge about the hotel and the locale. The last major event was 200 years ago, when the entire village burned down, so 1789 in Amsteg refers not to revolution but to the building of a new Stern und Post.

After swimming in the Golzernsee or walking in the Maderaner Valley, where better to write your postcards than in the small salon or *Stübli*, with Duke, the Bernese mountain dog, curled at your feet. Antiques abound, the bar is full of villagers and the restaurant looks over the garden and river. Bedrooms are all different but 'if your stay is short, opt for an older room, such as the single with the bed rescued from the fire. Not all of these have private bathrooms but who cares when you're surrounded by 200 years of history?' More refurbishing is planned.

Nearby St Gotthard Pass; walking.

6474 Amsteg UR
Tel (041) 8831440
Fax (041) 8830261
Location in middle of village; ample car parking, some covered
Meals breakfast, lunch, dinner
Prices rooms S-SSS
Rooms 15 double; 12 single; most have bath or shower; all have central heating, phone, radio
Facilities dining-room, sitting-room, bar, lift/elevator; terrace, garden
Credit cards AE, MC, V
Children very welcome
Disabled not suitable
Pets accepted
Closed Nov to Easter
Languages English, French, German, Italian, Spanish.
Proprietor Elisabeth Tresch

Central Cantons

Country inn, Gersau

Gasthaus Tübli

'This is the place for me, this is the real Switzerland' was the reaction to this chalet, and the delight of our inspector was shared by Thai television, who filmed a love story here. Dating from 1767, the house was completely renovated when the Schmid family took over in 1995. Thankfully, the traditional atmosphere persists, though the new yellow colour schemes enhance the walls and beams.

Andreas Schmid is the chef. His roots are in eastern Switzerland, but his cooking here is strictly central Swiss, with particular emphasis on fresh lake fish. His speciality, 'three fish on a plate', includes the salmon-like *Felchen*, *Egli* (perch) and *Seibling* (char). Most guests are families, or retired folk, who want to escape the pressures of modern life. That explains why there are no telephones or televisions in the bedrooms.

This small guest house on a quiet back street is not for everyone, however; those who want designer furnishings, Jacuzzis and the latest exercise equipment should look elsewhere. The small bedrooms and bathrooms are decidedly old-fashioned, just like the warmth of the welcome.

Nearby Lake Lucerne; walking.

6442 Gersau, Dorfstr 12 SZ
Tel (041) 841234
Fax (041) 841305
Location in heart of village, on north side of lake; ample car parking
Meals breakfast, lunch, dinner, snacks
Prices rooms SF45-200 with breakfast; DB&B from SF60; reduction for children; meals from SF15
Rooms 5 double; 2 family; all have bath or shower, central heating, phone; 1 single without private bath
Facilities dining-room, sitting-room, TV room; terrace, garden **Credit cards** AE, MC
Children very welcome
Disabled not suitable
Pets accepted
Closed restaurant only, Mon, Tues
Languages English, French, German
Proprietors Pasquale and Iris Proganó-Stockreiter

Central Cantons

Converted old house, Lucerne

Hofgarten

The best Swiss designers can combine ancient and modern without annoying fans of either period. This is a fine example of that skill. Although part of the city's oldest building, the hotel is hung with contemporary paintings from the collection in the Rebstock, its sister-establishment. Embedded in the walls are pieces of tile from the days when traditional ceramic ovens were produced here and five bedrooms still use these for back-up heating. All bedrooms, however, have modern furniture and decorations which together look like a work of art. Bathrooms 'make you want to get up early to make maximum use of everything they offer'. There are proper shaving mirrors, baths to stretch out in, big towels to curl up in, and plenty of natural light, thanks to glass walls and doors.

The restaurant also marries old and new: one area has linen table-cloths and crystal candelabra; another boasts a multi-hued ceramic ceiling and coloured crystal lights. Both offer vegetarian cooking that is delicious and original. Surrounded by flowers 'so fresh they must still be growing', our inspector was full of praise. 'What flair, what comfort, what peace, all in the heart of a city.'
Nearby central Lucerne; lake.

6006 Lucerne, Stadthofstr
14 L 6041 41 4108888
Tel (041) 4108888
Fax (041) 4108333
Location behind the Hotel Zum Rebstock; car parking on street
Meals breakfast, lunch, dinner, snacks
Prices rooms SS-SSS with breakfast
Rooms 16 double; 2 single; all have bath or shower, central heating, phone, TV, radio, minibar, hairdrier, safe
Facilities dining-room, sitting-room, bar, lift/elevator; terrace
Credit cards AE, DC, DC, V
Children welcome
Disabled not suitable
Pets accepted
Closed never
Languages English, French, German, Italian, Spanish
Manager Matthias Spitz

Central Cantons

Zum Rebstock

The owner of this 600-year-old hotel, Claudia Moser, is a master (or is it a mistress?) in the art of hotel-keeping. She is also an art lover, with 30 years' worth of collecting displayed on the walls.

Just as the paintings are original, so every room is different: here influenced by art deco, there a striking pink colour scheme. From the light fittings to the beds, even the telephones, nothing is uniform. 'It's not so unusual,' says Frau Moser, 'after all, is every room the same in your home?'

That sense of individuality continues with the food in each of the three restaurants. Eating here is like going to a dinner party every night, but always at the house of a first-rate cook. Nothing here is mass-produced, kept in the oven or created in large vats for diners with no taste buds. Local specialities are on the menu, including Lucerne's own *Chügeli-Pastete* (*vol-au-vent*). The breakfast buffet shows the same care. No plastic pots of yoghurt or curled-up cheese; instead, ten different sorts of fresh bread, fresh orange juice, a heap of ripe strawberries and your own fresh coffee. 'I could go on for ever,' enthused our inspector. 'Go and see for yourself.'

Nearby lake.

6006 Lucerne, St Leodegarstr 3 LU
Tel (041) 4103581
Fax (041) 4103917
Location in heart of Lucerne; car parking in street
Meals breakfast, lunch, dinner, snacks
Prices rooms SS-SSS with breakfast
Rooms 23 double; 5 single; all have bath or shower, central heating, phone, TV, radio, minibar, hairdrier

Facilities 3 dining-rooms, sitting-room, bar, TV room lift/elevator; terrace
Credit cards AE, DC, MC, V
Children welcome
Disabled not suitable
Pets accepted
Closed never
Languages English, French, German, Italian
Proprietor Claudia Moser

Central Cantons

Waldhaus

'The definitive Swiss view' declared our inspector as he stood on the terrace, stunned by the 180° panorama. To the left are the mountains above Altdorf at the end of the lake, then the Gotthard, Titlis, Jochpass, and Engelberg, with Pilatus towering above on the right. At sunset, the snowy peaks change to twinkling lights and the floodlit summit of Pilatus seems to have taken off and be hovering above your right shoulder.

Built over a century ago but with subsequent additions, the Waldhaus is no architectural gem. The Galliker family, who bought the property in 1990, concentrated first on improving the kitchen; they have succeeded. 'My home-made ravioli with leek and the freshest of fish (although the hotel does have its own smoke-house for salmon) are the only thing that took my eyes away from the view.' The next stage is upgrading the bedrooms which are acceptable if not memorable, except when you look out of the window. In winter, skiing is only 30 minutes away. In summer, guests swim in the pool, jog through the trees, or stroll through the park. 'Do take breakfast on the terrace with the sun rising above the snow-capped peaks. Worth the entire journey.'
Nearby Pilatus, Lucerne; hiking.

6048 Horw-Lucerne, auf Oberrüti LU
Tel (041) 3491500
Fax (041) 3491515
Location on Horw peninsula; ample car parking
Meals breakfast, lunch, dinner, snacks
Prices rooms S-SSS with breakfast
Rooms 11 double; 6 single; all have bath or shower, central heating, phone, TV, radio, minibar
Facilities dining-room, sitting-room, bar; terrace, garden, swimming-pool
Credit cards AE, DC, MC, V
Children welcome
Disabled not suitable
Pets accepted
Closed Feb; restaurant only, Mon; Tues in winter
Languages English, French, German, Italian, Spanish
Proprietors Galliker family

Central Cantons

Country house hotel, Meggen

Balm

Herr Stofer, the owner since 1969, has done every job in the hotel business and has worked all over the world. No wonder he has strong views. Rule one is that the customer may not always be right and that, as a professional, he knows what a good hotel needs. Or does not need. 'Carpets,' he declares, 'hold dirt and are impossible to clean properly, unlike proper, polished-wood floors which show every speck of dust. Both guest and management can see when they are spick and span.' So, only the few very creaky bedroom floors are covered. Minibars? Who needs them when someone is on hand to bring you a drink or a bottle of water? On our first visit, televisions were banned, but times change. Renovations in 1995 produced new bedrooms – with TV. Single rooms were converted so that all rooms now have smart bathrooms. Readers approve, saying that the changes are more 'relaxing'. And relaxing is easy when you are surrounded by trees and flowers, with a terrace overlooking the garden and lawns sweeping down to the distant lake. Additions to the north and south side of the hotel have not affected the restaurant where the motto is 'Business as usual'. Some things, thankfully, never change.

Nearby Rigi; Lucerne, Lake Lucerne, water-sports.

6045 Meggen LU
Tel (041) 3771135
Fax (041) 3772383
Location off main road outside Meggen; ample car parking
Meals breakfast, lunch, dinner, snacks
Prices rooms S-SSS with breakfast
Rooms 18 double; most have bath or shower; all have central heating, phone, TV, radio

Facilities dining-room, sitting-room, bar, lift/elevator; terrace, garden
Credit cards AE, DC, MC, V
Children welcome
Disabled not suitable
Pets accepted
Closed Jan
Languages English, French, German, Italian
Proprietors Stofer-Sigrist family

Central Cantons

Town hotel, Schwyz

Wysses Rössli

This ancient town saw the origins of the Swiss Federation in 1291. The hotel is newer, dating from the 17thC, but 20 years ago it burnt to the ground. Rebuilt, it still has a prime position on the stunning main square but inside, the look is more 1960s than 1640s, particularly in the entrance and sitting area. Here, tiled floors and white walls are rather clinical, as if catering more to a business than holiday clientele. Having taken over, the Ming-Odermatts are working hard to put back some Swiss hospitality and even warmth into the place. They have succeeded already in the informal bar-restaurant which is popular and full of locals.

Although bedrooms are bland, with furniture designed more for convenience than for comfort, mattresses are excellent. In fact, our inspector overslept; he assumed the bells of the church opposite would wake him early in the morning but they sounded 'like a grandfather clock in the hall'. Bathrooms are 'wash and go' with towels not fluffy but 'rather harsh, perhaps to match the carpet'. Corner bedrooms, such as number 416, have views of the mountains as well as the old town, which is even more atmospheric when the sightseers have gone home.

Nearby Swiss Federation memorials and museums; Lake Lucerne.

6430 Schwyz SZ
Tel (041) 8111922
Fax (041) 8111046
Location on the Hauptplatz, in the middle of town; ample car parking in town square
Meals breakfast, lunch, dinner, snacks
Prices rooms SS-SSS with breakfast; DB&B from SF120; reduction for children; meals from SF16
Rooms 21 double; 5 single; all have bath or shower, central heating, phone, TV, radio, minibar
Facilities 3 dining-rooms, sitting-room, bar, lift/elevator; terrace, garden
Credit cards AE, DC, MC, V
Children welcome
Disabled reasonable access
Pets accepted
Closed Christmas, New Year
Languages English, French, German, Italian
Proprietors Urs and Ruth Ming-Odermatt

Central Cantons

Lakeside hotel, Weggis

Seehof/Hotel Du Lac

The Hotel du Lac is like an old friend who has been here for over 150 years, looking after generations of families taking their annual holiday in the mountains. Weggis offers almost as much to fans of water sports as it does to walkers and climbers, and this inn is right on the lake. The main draws are the location, right in the heart of town, and the large, lakeside terrace. Inside, there is no single style of furnishings; when work needs to be done, or a room redecorated, the Zimmermans get on with it.

The more expensive bedrooms overlook the water but the cheaper ones at the back have a fine view of the Rigi and are quiet enough since most road traffic uses the bypass. 'Functional' describes the tables, chairs and neutral colours. Bathrooms often suffer from being fitted into corners and two bedrooms do not have private facilities. British regulars are among the loyal clientele who are fond of this staid old lady, a friendly soul who welcomes you to her rather dark interior and, in the restaurant with its lovely view, offers her speciality: fish fondue. Like many things that grandmothers make, it is not nearly as strange as it sounds.
Nearby Lake Lucerne, water sports; walking, Rigi.

6353 Weggis LU
Tel (041) 3901151
Fax (041) 3901119
Location on north side of lake; limited car parking
Meals breakfast, lunch, dinner, snacks
Prices rooms S-SSS with breakfast
Rooms 25 double; most have bath or shower; all have phone, TV, radio, minibar, safe
Facilities dining-room, sitting-room, lift/elevator, TV room; terrace, garden
Credit cards AE, DC, MC, V
Children very welcome
Disabled not suitable
Pets accepted
Closed Nov, Dec
Languages English, French, German, Italian
Proprietors Toni and Verena Zimmermann

NE Cantons

Appenzell

Usually, we are suspicious of hotels that drape themselves in flags but the Appenzell's decorations are all part of the extraordinary main square of a town famous for its multi-coloured houses. The checkerboard façade of butter-yellow and purple, the silhouettes of medieval townsfolk and those long banners are part and parcel of the Appenzell effect.

It would be easy to cash in on the regular flow of camera-carrying tourists by running a hotel that is merely adequate, but Margrit and Leo Sutter have worked hard to make this a special place. On the ground floor is Leo's popular *Konditorei*, full of home-made temptations such as *Biberli* and *Züngli* (local cookies), cakes, ice-cream and jellied fruit confections. In summer, visitors sit outside beneath striped sunshades, lunching on salads, trout, pork chops and vegetarian risottos, perhaps with a glass of freshly-pressed strawberry and pear juice. In the evening, the restaurant inside has more sophisticated fare and, of course, Leo's desserts. Bedrooms were imaginatively redecorated in 1992 using soft blues, pinks and greens, while the small bathrooms were updated. All in all, quite a find.

Nearby winter sports; hiking, swimming-pools, tennis.

Landsgemeindeplatz, 9050 Appenzell AI
Tel (071) 7874211
Fax (071) 7874284
E-mail info@hotel-appenzell.ch
Location on main square; own car parking nearby
Meals breakfast, lunch, dinner, snacks
Prices rooms S-SS with breakfast
Rooms 16 double; all have bath or shower, central heating, phone, TV, radio, minibar
Facilities dining-room, sitting-room, lift/elevator; terrace
Credit cards AE, DC, MC, V
Children welcome
Disabled 2 bedrooms with wheelchair access
Pets accepted
Closed Nov
Languages English, French, German, Italian
Proprietors Sutter family

NE Cantons

Ancient inn, Appenzell

Säntis

'We never stop making improvements,' claims Stefan Heeb, the owner of the best-known inn in the region. Although the outside looks antique, with its red, black and yellow patterns, the interior has been rebuilt and enlarged over the years. When the Heeb family took over in 1919, it was little more than a guest-house. 'This was once the stables,' he explains with a chuckle, waving towards the large reception area with its stone floor, Persian carpets, inviting sofas and red-painted beams.

In the low-ceilinged restaurant, small, white-curtained windows overlook the square, while pictures of Herr Heeb's parents flank a wood-carving of Appenzell in 1800. Staff in long black skirts and bold, floral-print blouses serve specialities such as lamb and lake fish, plus sausage that is a mixture of beef and pork. On the cheeseboard, what else but local cheeses such as the strongly-flavoured, hard *Rässkäse*, matured for four months. There are even Appenzell wines: a Blauburgunder from the Rhine Valley and a Riesling/Sylvaner from Innerrhoden. Of the bedrooms, number 242 is particularly popular thanks to its four-poster bed, hung with frilly, white curtains.

Nearby winter sports; hiking, swimming-pools, tennis.

am Landsgemeindeplatz, 9050 Appenzell AI
Tel (071) 7881111
Fax (071) 7881110
E-mail romantikhotelsaentis@bluewin.ch
Location on main square; own car parking
Meals breakfast, lunch, dinner, snacks
Prices rooms SS-SSS with breakfast
Rooms 32 double; 4 single; all have bath or shower, central heating, phone, TV, radio, minibar
Facilities 3 dining-rooms, sitting-room, bar, lift/elevator; terrace, garden
Credit cards AE, DC, MC, V
Children welcome
Disabled reasonable access
Pets accepted
Closed mid-Jan to end Feb
Languages English, French, German, Italian
Proprietors Heeb family

NE Cantons

Boutique brewery, Arbon am Bodensee

Gasthof Frohsinn

This is a must for beer fans, and anyone else wanting something out of the ordinary. The Surbeck family are not just hoteliers, they are brewers. Down in the basement, the beer cellar has a vaulted roof dating from medieval times, wooden benches and a sprinkling of locals, even early in the morning. Sacks full of barley stand ready for the two copper mash tuns, or vats, presided over by the brew master. Twice a week, 500 litres of lager are produced, with a stronger brown beer made in winter as well. Sample the cooking, particularly the vegetarian and stir-fry dishes, of the assistant chef and then head for the *Kegelbahnen*. 'Previous experience of 10-pin bowling will not make you an expert,' warns our inspector, whose attempts to control the ball met with failure. 'Swallow your pride, buy a round of Frohsinn beer and ask the regulars for advice.'

As for the rest of the hotel, bedrooms are small, neat and plain; 'strictly for sleeping' as the bathrooms (most with shower only) are just for a quick wash. The main dining-room is modern, where chef Martin Surbeck shows off his highly-rated skills. Large windows have views over vineyards towards the lake.

Nearby lake, vineyards.

9320 Arbon,
Romanshornerstr 15 TG
Tel (071) 4478484
Fax (071) 4464142
Location in village; ample car parking
Meals breakfast, lunch, dinner, snacks
Prices rooms SS-SSS with breakfast
Rooms 8 double; 3 single; all have bath or shower, central heating, phone, TV, radio, minibar

Facilities 2 dining-rooms, bar; terrace, garden
Credit cards AE, DC, MC, V
Children welcome
Disabled not suitable
Pets accepted
Closed never; restaurant only, Sun, Mon
Languages English, French, German, Italian
Proprietors Simone and Martin Surbeck

NE Cantons

Riverside hotel, Gottlieben near Kreuzlingen

Krone

Many people would be happy to pay to walk round this village whose history dates back to the 12thC. The narrow lanes and half-timbered houses, dominated by the monastery, stand right on the bank of the River Rhine, between the Bodensee and the smaller Untersee. Luckily, there are other photogenic gems in Switzerland so this one has not been over-visited and still feels like a living town, not a tourist attraction.

Experienced hotel-keepers, the Schraner-Michaelis settled here some 18 years ago and have stamped their personalities on this 300-year old inn. They delight in showing guests around. 'Take the tour before deciding on a bedroom' recommended our inspector, who found those in the modern extension at the back rather dark and plain. 'Perhaps that's because I saw the glorious rooms at the front first' he admitted. These have heavy classical furniture, fabric-covered walls and the river rolling by outside. The best is luxurious and worth the extra expense for a romantic weekend. Our man liked the restaurant, 'like a gentle-men's club, all polished dark wood' and the exquisite breakfast room. Verdict: 'comfort, peace and tranquillity'.

Nearby the town of Constance and the lake.

8274 Gottlieben TG
Tel (071) 6668060
Fax (071) 6668069
E-mail krone@romantikhotel.ch
Location in village; limited car parking on quayside
Meals breakfast, lunch, dinner, snacks
Prices rooms SS-SSS with breakfast
Rooms 19 double; 4 single; 2 suites; all have bath or shower, central heating, phone, TV, radio, minibar

Facilities dining-room, lift/elevator; terrace
Credit cards AE, DC, MC, V
Children welcome
Disabled not suitable
Pets accepted
Closed never
Languages English, French, German, Italian
Proprietors Schraner-Michaeli family

NE Cantons

Lakeside villa, Bottighofen

Schlössli Bottighofen

'A pity about the 1960s concrete apartment blocks' commented our inspector, who advises guests to ignore these unattractive buildings as they drive down the narrow lane to the lake. On the shore, by itself, stands this delightful 'small castle' built in the 1640s. Once the pride of the Bishop of Constance, various additions have been made by subsequent owners, one of whom was the Pernod of Pernod fame.

When our reporter arrived, groups of genteel ladies were enjoying lunch in the Schifferstube, an informal restaurant, popular for a drink as well as for meals. This opens on to the tree-shaded terrace and garden, right at the water's edge, with views of sailboats and the small yacht harbour where boats may be hired. Upstairs is the gourmet restaurant and also the pretty bedrooms, each with a different look. 'Understated luxury' should be the motto of Bruno Lüthy, who has chosen fabrics and carpets in subtle patterns that look more like a private home than a hotel. Bathrooms, too, show careful planning; some are on the small side, but every bit of space is used and pink marble wash-basins make a change from the usual white.

Nearby lake and town of Constance.

8598 Bottighofen TG
Tel (071) 6881275
Fax (071) 6881540
Location on lake; ample car parking
Meals breakfast, lunch, dinner, snacks
Prices rooms SS-SSS with breakfast
Rooms 10 double; 1 single; all have bath or shower, central heating, phone, TV, radio, minibar
Facilities 2 dining-rooms; terrace
Credit cards AE, DC, MC, V
Children welcome
Disabled not suitable
Pets accepted
Closed never
Languages English, French, German, Italian
Proprietor Bruno Lüthy

NE Cantons

Lakeside hotel, Mannenbach

Schiff

Most members of the *Landgasthof* association are old wayside inns, so the totally modern Schiff comes as a shock, particularly in this area known for its ancient half-timbered buildings. Set on the shore of the Untersee, 'this is more like a Mediterranean hotel', according to our inspector, who picked out the quarry-tiled floor, port-hole windows in reception and plain white plaster walls as examples of a 'seaside feel'.

Only fifteen years old, the terracotta stucco building with its pale pine balconies is shaded by mature chestnut trees, while the restaurant and terrace look on to the water. Swans paddling past moored motor and sailing boats complete the idyllic scene. With the ferry stop nearby and the cycle path at the door, the Schiff makes a popular stop on a day out but the cooking has a fine reputation, offering fish from the lake such as pike, carp and perch. Fish soup is featured daily, while Mannenbach's own vineyards provide the ideal accompaniment, a chilled bottle of Riesling/Sylvaner. Bedrooms are light, bright and neat: white walls, yellow pine and golden candlewick bedspreads complete the holiday atmosphere.

Nearby vineyards, lake, Napoleon Museum.

8268 Mannenbach am
Untersee TG
Tel (071) 6634141
Fax (071) 6634150
E-mail seehotel-schiff@swissonline.ch
Location on lake; ample car parking
Meals breakfast, lunch, dinner, snacks
Prices rooms SS-SSS with breakfast
Rooms 18 double; all have bath or shower, central heating, phone, radio; TV

by request
Facilities 2 dining-rooms, sitting-room, bar, lift/elevator; terrace, garden
Credit cards AE, DC, MC, V
Children very welcome
Disabled good access
Pets accepted
Closed mid-Feb
Languages English, French, German
Manager Knup family

NE Cantons

Lakeside hotel, Rapperswil

Schwanen

Although these particular Swans have been in the same family for over 30 years, only recently have they thrown off the dark plumage of a cygnet and, after renovation, revealed themselves as elegant adults. Large and imposing, the hotel dominates the middle of town, in front of the castle and overlooking the lake. Much space is devoted to banqueting and meeting rooms for companies from Zurich and although our inspector found the restaurants rather impersonal, he liked the less formal bistro-bar with its high ceilings, terrace and innovative menu.

At the back of the bar, glass doors lead to a gallery showing the work of local artists. This is the idea of Margrit Riva, who believes the hotel should be part of the community. Her interest in design ensured that the conversion from old to new retained the character of the building, but in a striking format. Corridors and bedrooms are furnished in dramatic black and white. 'I loved it but some people won't' commented our inspector, who was even more impressed by the split-level suite. Climb the spiral staircase to the bedroom under the eaves and its circular bathroom with windows overlooking the lake.

Nearby old town, lake.

8640 Rapperswil SG
Tel (055) 2208500
Fax (055) 2107777
Location by lake; ample car parking
Meals breakfast, lunch, dinner, snacks
Prices rooms S-SSSS, breakfast extra
Rooms 15 double; 3 single; 1 suite; all have bath or shower, central heating, phone, TV, radio, minibar, hairdrier, safe
Facilities 3 dining-rooms, sitting-room, bar, lift/elevator; terrace
Credit cards AE, DC, MC, V
Children welcome
Disabled not suitable
Pets accepted
Closed never
Languages English, French, German, Italian, Spanish
Proprietors Margrit and Quirino Riva

NE Cantons

Riverside hotel, Schaffhausen

Rheinhotel Fischerzunft

What was once the Fishermen's Guildhall of Schaffhausen is now one of the most famous restaurants in Switzerland. In 1975, André Jaeger returned from the Peninsula Hotel in Hong Kong to take over the family business. Since then he has developed a cuisine that is a 'perfect blend of East and West'. Marinated salmon with Teriyaki sauce, perch-pike fillet with curry sauce and home-made mango chutney, and spring chicken 'yin and yang' with sweet ginger and orange sauce were just a few dishes on a menu of 'such stunning originality that I want to eat it all'. The presentation is a photographic dream.

Our inspector was also impressed by the restaurant itself: enough space between tables for private conversations, beautiful flowers and distinctive floral print table-cloths. 'No pale blues and pinks here; this is a design statement.' Bedrooms show the same flair. The more expensive have a river view but all are deeply comfortable, with individual colour themes for paintwork, fabrics and carpets. Chinese prints abound, looking surprisingly natural even on candy-stripe wallpaper. 'Total perfection' was the verdict; but book your table when reserving a room.

Nearby Rhine Falls, Munot Castle, old town.

8200 Schaffhausen, Rheinquai 8 SH
Tel (052) 6320505
Fax (052) 6320513
E-mail fischerzunft@relaischateaux.fr
Location on river bank, own car parking
Meals breakfast, lunch, dinner
Prices rooms SSS-SSSS with breakfast
Rooms 10 double; all have bath or shower, central heating, phone, TV, radio, minibar, hairdrier, safe
Facilities dining-room, sitting-room; terrace
Credit cards AE, DC, MC, V
Children welcome but not suitable
Disabled not suitable
Pets accepted
Closed never; restaurant only, Tue
Languages English, French, German, Italian, Spanish
Proprietor André Jaeger

NE Cantons

Suburban hotel, Schaffhausen

Park Villa

'This could be a set for one of Alfred Hitchcock's films.' That was the first impression of this house, whose steep roof, gables and stone façade look rather forbidding. 'Don't let that put you off, though' pleaded our inspector. Built in 1900 by a banker, it had become a pension when Max Schlumpf bought it and restored the look and ambience of a private home, albeit one of a rather eccentric grandfather. Forget the standardisation of hotel chains; from the minute you step into the dark, high-ceilinged entrance, with its sweeping wooden staircase and stuffed tiger, you know this hotel is one of a kind.

The bar is in the former library while the white-walled breakfast-room has large, arched windows looking into the garden. There are parquet floors, patterned carpets and most of the furniture is old, if not antique.

The size of bedrooms varies enormously; those in the attic are small, cosy and more simply decorated than larger ones below. You may get a bed dating from 1829 or a carved four-poster, but train-spotters should ask for one of the corner rooms where they can focus their binoculars on the nearby railway line.

Nearby Rhine Falls, Munot Castle, old city.

8200 Schaffhausen, Parkstr 18 SH
Tel (052) 6252737
Fax (052) 6241253
Location in parkland above railway line; own car parking
Meals breakfast, lunch, dinner, snacks
Prices rooms S-SSS with breakfast
Rooms 15 double; 7 single; most have bath or shower, central heating, phone, TV, radio, minibar, hairdrier

Facilities 2 dining-rooms, sitting-room, bar; terrace, garden, tennis court
Credit cards AE, DC, MC, V
Children welcome
Disabled not suitable
Pets accepted
Closed never
Languages English, French, German, Italian
Proprietor Max Schlumpf

NE Cantons

Mountain hotel, Abtwil

Säntisblick

A sense of adventure is needed to find this hotel, perched high on a hill above St Gallen and looking down on Abtwil. From this village, drive uphill, first through seemingly endless suburbia and then fields. Persevere, despite the absence of signs; the reward is a country inn set among farms. These provide horses for riding and there are even hitching rings at the side of the hotel. You don't need to hitch your children to anything, however; they can run freely or climb in the adventure playground.

Hugo Graber and his family came here in 1987 and established a homey atmosphere that has proved popular with the locals. Walk through the small bar into the restaurant or onto the terrace where there are regular barbecues in fine weather. From both, the panorama is breath-taking: the entire Säntis region spread out below. The century-old house has been modernised but still has plenty of wood. Bedrooms are not luxurious but have a surprising level of facilities such as video recorders and well-stocked cosmetic cabinets in the bathrooms. Although simple and ideal for families, our reporter thought the prices a bit expensive. Perhaps you are paying for the view.

Nearby St Gallen and Lake Constance.

9030 Abtwil-St Gallen,
Grimmstr SG
Tel (071) 3132525
Fax (071) 3132526
Location on hillside among farms; ample car parking
Meals breakfast, lunch, dinner, snacks
Prices rooms SS-SSS with breakfast
Rooms 11 double; 4 single; all have bath or shower, central heating, phone, TV, radio, minibar, hairdrier

Facilities 2 dining-rooms, sitting-room, lift/elevator; terrace, garden
Credit cards AE, DC, MC, V
Children very welcome
Disabled not suitable
Pets accepted
Closed never; restaurant only, Mon
Languages English, French, German, Italian
Proprietor Hugo Graber

NE Cantons

Modern lakeside hotel, Steckborn

Feldbach

If you were told to turn off the main road, walk through a boat yard and look at a hotel built in 1986 would you bother? Luckily, our reporter did and was bowled over by this converted 13thC convent which 'deserves a feature in a design and architecture magazine'. Much was demolished in 1798 but the outbuildings, set among gardens on the shore of the lake, survive. So does the refectory, with its onion-domed tower which houses the restaurant and bar. Across the courtyard, a glass-walled walkway gives this two-storey building the look of a medieval cloister and the colonnaded entrance 'looks like a church'.

Bedrooms are all the same, of adequate size, with simple furniture and just a touch of colour in the duvets. This is one hotel where disabled travellers will have no difficulty negotiating corridors and a wide lift/elevator gives access to the floor above. Up a ramp is a convent garden complete with fountain and scented flowers. With not a fence or gate in sight, you feel part of the surrounding park. This is an extraordinary and harmonious mix of ancient and ultra-modern that is 'ideal for everyone from nine months to ninety years'. Free bicycles for guests.

Nearby ferry stop, Lake Constance.

8266 Steckborn TG
Tel (052) 7622121
Fax (052) 7622191
E-mail feldbach@active.ch
Location on lake in park land; own car parking
Meals breakfast, lunch, dinner, snacks
Prices rooms SS-SSSS with breakfast
Rooms 36 double; all have bath or shower, central heating, phone, radio, minibar; TV on request

Facilities dining-room, sitting-room, bar, sauna, fitness area, lift/elevator; terrace, garden
Credit cards AE, DC, MC, V
Children very welcome
Disabled excellent access
Pets accepted
Closed never
Languages English, French, German, Italian
Manager Daniel Füglister

NE Cantons

Ancient hostelry, Stein am Rhein

Rheinfels

Stein am Rhein is such a touristy town that many travellers avoid its narrow streets and ancient buildings altogether. The secret, of course, is to stay overnight; then you can enjoy the medieval atmosphere when the day-trippers have gone home.

The Rheinfels sits on the riverbank next to the bridge; its terrace restaurant overhangs the water where ducks and swans amuse the diners who flock to enjoy Edi Schwegler's cooking. Whether it is fillets of sander, served with a delicate sorrel sauce, or char from the Rhine itself, Edi has a sure touch with fish. An avid hunter, he also serves game in season. The hotel itself is like a huge wooden galleon turned upside down, with stately timbers supporting the curved roof. Climb the stairs, which creak with every step, and full-size suits of armour and stuffed birds stare silently across the landing. Some of the bedrooms have been refurbished recently. Number 35 at the top, for example, has rosebud-patterned wallpaper, pink duvets and dark, old beams. A map of the village as it was in 1662 shows each house clearly numbered. The tiny windows look down to the river and bridge. All in all, the hotel maintains its medieval feel.

Nearby old city, lake.

8260 Stein am Rhein SH
Tel (052) 7412144
Fax (052) 7412522
Location overlooking river; car parking nearby
Meals breakfast, lunch, dinner, snacks
Prices rooms SS with breakfast
Rooms 17 double; all have bath or shower, central heating, phone, TV, radio, minibar
Facilities 4 dining-rooms,

sitting-room, bar; terrace
Credit cards AE, DC, MC, V
Children welcome
Disabled not suitable
Pets accepted
Closed Jan, Feb; restaurant only, Thurs
Languages English, French, German, Italian
Proprietors Schwegler-Wick family

Liechtenstein

Gasthof Löwen

A century ago, travellers agreed that 'if you stop in Liechtenstein, you have to stay at the Löwen.' Thanks to careful and expensive restoration, that advice holds true again. This is, perhaps, the oldest inn in the country, having stood on the main road between Germany and Italy since medieval days. Now it is almost a living museum. 'The poet, Goethe, ate badly here but we have changed the chef,' quipped Fritz Gantenbein as he pointed out the 400-year-old fresco in the dining room, the intricately-painted ceiling that renovations uncovered in the elegant *Johannes-Stube*, and the tale of the Niebelungen carved into the panelling of the *Lucretia-Stube*.

White walls and parquet floors provide a simple backdrop for antiques and oriental carpets. On one floor, bedrooms are named after women, on another for men; many have matching massive carved wooden beds and armoires.

Bathrooms are magnificently modern with plush towels, white marble and excellent lighting. Rooms overlooking the road can be noisy in summer with the windows open; those at the back face the garden and vineyards.

Nearby Vaduz castle, national museum; winter sports, hiking.

Herrengasse 35,
9490 Vaduz FL
Tel (0423) 2381144
Fax (0423) 2381145
E-mail loewen@hotels.li
Location on main road on edge of Vaduz; ample car parking
Meals breakfast, lunch, dinner, snacks
Prices rooms SS-SSSS with breakfast
Rooms 6 double; 1 single; all have bath or shower, central heating, phone, TV, radio, minibar, hairdrier
Facilities 2 dining-rooms, sitting-room, bar; terrace, garden,
Credit cards AE, DC, MC, V
Children welcome
Disabled not suitable
Pets accepted
Closed Christmas, New Year
Languages English, French, German, Italian
Manager Fritz Gantenbein

Liechtenstein

Real

Vaduz has two famous enterprises run by Reals. 'For my uncle at the Sonnenhof, the hotel is the priority; for us, it is the restaurant,' explained Martin Real, who took time off to see the world before coming home to take over as chef from his father, Félix. Their 'hotel, café, restaurant' may look ordinary from the street but inside is the best cuisine in the principality. Locals know that you can eat the same dishes in the ground-floor brasserie as in the 'Restaurant Au Premier' upstairs. That means classic French cooking with a modern twist: Creole *pot au feu* with lobster broth or scampi with lemon noodles. Martin takes pride in his own smoked venison, pork and even Scotch salmon, while the wine-list includes bottles from the family's vineyard and their own *marc*.

The look is sober, conservative and masculine, to suit the mainly business clientele. The collection of cockerels, however, belongs to Martin's mother; there is even a rooster on the menu covers. As for bedrooms, these are comfortable, if unremarkable. All have 'cosmetic bars', filled with toiletries, toothbrushes and combs. Those at the back are quieter.

Nearby Vaduz castle, museums; winter sports.

9490 Vaduz FL
Tel (0423) 2322222
Fax (0423) 2320891
E-mail real@hotels.li
Location in middle of Vaduz, on main road; own car parking
Meals breakfast, lunch, dinner, snacks
Prices rooms SS-SSS with breakfast; meals from SF80
Rooms 6 double; 4 single; all have bath or shower, central heating, phone, TV, radio, minibar, hairdrier, safe; some air-conditioning
Facilities dining-room, sitting-room, bar, lift/elevator; terrace
Credit cards AE, DC, MC, V
Children not suitable
Disabled reasonable access
Pets accepted
Closed Christmas
Languages English, French, German, Italian
Proprietors Real family

Liechtenstein

Sonnenhof

'Total seclusion and a perfect view of Vaduz Castle' wrote our inspector as she stood in the gardens and surveyed the principality, spread over the hills and the valley below. Emil Real, the brother of Félix at the Restaurant Real in Vaduz, bought a small *pension* in 1963, then gradually expanded and improved the facilities. The box-like architecture of that era looks rather dated and functional nowadays but there are some cosy corners, such as the *Stübli*, a glassed-in former terrace, and the *Kaminzimmer*, with its fireplace, books and squashy leather sofas and armchairs. A large, stained-glass onion panel decorates the dining-room which is the show-case for Emil's culinary talents and is reserved for those staying at the hotel.

Bedrooms are large enough for a sitting area by the picture windows plus a bench long enough for three big suitcases. On the ground floor, sliding doors open into the garden; upstairs, there are balconies. Our reporter, who is partial to hotels with swimming-pools, thought the trapeze suspended above the water looked like fun. 'Very comfortable, away from it all but a sombre interior. Fine for bankers but rather dull for holiday-makers.'
Nearby Vaduz and its museums; walks, winter-sports.

9490 Vaduz FL
Tel (0423) 2321192
Fax (0423) 2320053
Location on quiet, residential hillside above Vaduz; ample car parking, garage
Meals breakfast, lunch, dinner, snacks
Prices rooms SSS-SSSS with breakfast
Rooms 10 double; 7 single; 12 suites; all have bath or shower, central heating, phone, TV, radio, minibar, hairdrier, safe **Facilities** 2 dining-rooms, 2 sitting-rooms, bar, sauna and fitness area, lift/elevator; terrace, garden, indoor swimming-pool
Credit cards AE, DC, MC, V
Children not suitable
Disabled good access
Pets accepted **Closed** 20 Dec to 6 Jan; restaurant only, 20 Dec to 1 Mar
Languages English, French, German, Italian
Proprietors Real family

Graubünden

Belri

'A former girls' finishing school, but don't let that put you off' was
the intriguing beginning of the report on this converted chalet,
opposite the local museum right at the top of Arosa. 'Like a great-
aunt's house' was the comment on the interior, particularly the
dark wood-panelled hall and wide staircase that creaks with every
step. Upstairs, the students in number 38 probably lay awake in
their twin four-poster beds, staring at the carved partridge on the
ceiling, while those in number 43, no doubt preferred sitting on
the roof-top terrace to studying at the jolly red-painted desk and
chairs. In contrast to this   remembrance of things past is the
spacious, contemporary comfort of the new suite with its eau-de-
Nil carpet, pretty white organdie curtains and pale wood. There
are also five functional bedrooms in the new wing, to be redecorated in 1994.

This is one hotel where the claim of 'ski out, ski back' really is
justified and lifts to the Weisshorn and the Hörnli are only minutes away. At the end of the day, there are three Stüblis for relaxation and socialising . 'The old-fashioned ambience of a New
England inn' was the comment of one American visitor.
Nearby downhill skiing, hiking.

7050 Innerarosa, Arosa GR
Tel (081) 3771716
Fax (081) 3774075
Location at top of Arosa in
Innerarosa; ample car
parking, 8 garages
Meals breakfast only, summer;
breakfast, lunch, dinner,
snacks in winter
Prices rooms S-SS with
breakfast (summer); DB&B
from SS (winter)
Rooms 12 double; 5 single; 1
suite; all have bath or shower,
central heating, phone, TV,
radio
Facilities dining-room, 3
sitting-rooms
Credit cards MC, V
Children very welcome,
Disabled not suitable
Pets accepted
Closed Nov to mid-Dec; after
Easter to late June
Languages English, French,
German, Italian
Managers Beerli family

Graubünden

❉ Historic house, Bever ❉

Chesa Salis

'Worth a whole roll of film' trumpeted the report on this house that dates back to the 16thC but was embellished by the patrician Salis family who bought it in 1870. 'It's old, it's not practical but we love it,' says Betty Jösler, who with her husband, Carlos, has managed the hotel since 1985. Before that it was a bed-and-breakfast but now the restaurant has a fine reputation. 'We are away from the village, we don't have a swimming-pool, so we spoil our guests with good food.' Carlos is in charge of the kitchen and menus include local as well as classic French and Italian dishes. The dining-room was once the entrance and the carved front door remains, matched by an elaborate wrought-iron gate. Off to one side is a small room for private parties that is 'like a doll's house, completely wood-panelled, with book-shelves, an escritoire and tiny windows'.

Some of the bedrooms have a similar atmosphere, particularly number 35, where the wood is painted like a music box. Right at the top is number 44, where tall folk have to be careful of the low beams, even in the bathroom. 'If only grandma's house had looked like this' was our reporter's final comment.

Nearby winter sports; hiking, mountain-biking.

7502 Bever GR
Tel (081) 8524838
Fax (081) 8524706
E-mail chesa.salis@compunet.ch
Location on the edge of the village; ample car parking, some covered
Meals breakfast, lunch, dinner, snacks
Prices rooms SS-SSS with breakfast
Rooms 20 double; all have bath or shower, central heating, phone, TV, radio

Facilities 3 dining-rooms, sitting-room, lift/elevator; terrace, garden
Credit cards AE, DC, MC, V
Children welcome
Disabled not suitable
Pets accepted; stables for horses
Closed mid-Oct to mid-Dec; after Easter to mid-June
Languages English, French, German, Italian
Managers Betty and Carlos Jösler

Graubünden

❋ **Old house, Celerina** ❋

Chesa Rosatsch

Just below St Mortiz, the village of Celerina is an ideal base to explore the famous ski runs in winter, or the walks along the Engadine Valley in summer. Down a quiet side street, an ornate sign marks the 300-year-old Chesa Rosatsch, right by the Inn River. In 1996, what was already a comfortable, family-run hotel was upgraded even further by the new managers. In recent years, expansion has doubled the number of bedrooms, but the 'small' and 'charming' ambience remains. The cheerful, primrose yellow annexe has the same deep windows and sloping roof as its ancient neighbour and, by using natural materials such as untreated wood, stone and linen, the effect is traditional with a modern twist. Colours are bolder and brighter, too. Overall, our readers approve of the changes, which include the restaurants. The Stüvas, with its mellow wood-panelling and ornate door-lock, had always been a meeting place for villagers and holiday makers alike. Now it is dedicated to lighter, gourmet dishes, while the more informal La Cuort is an indoor courtyard, with a wood-fired oven. The Inn Bar, with its array of malt whiskies and cigars, has become a fashionable spot.

Nearby downhill skiing; cross country; hiking.

7505 Celerina GR
Tel (081) 8370101
Fax (081) 8370100
E-mail hotel@rosatsch.ch
Location on edge of village, by river; ample car parking
Meals breakfast, lunch, dinner, snacks
Prices rooms SS-SSSS with breakfast
Rooms 35 double; all have bath or shower, central heating, phone, TV, radio, hairdrier, minibar, safe

Facilities 4 dining-rooms, sitting-room, bar; terrace, sauna
Credit cards AE, DC, MC, V
Children very welcome
Disabled not suitable
Pets accepted
Closed mid-Apr to mid-Jun; mid-Oct to mid-Dec
Languages English, French, German, Italian
Proprietors Doris and Christian Caflisch

Graubünden

❊ **Village inn, Celerina** ❊

Stüvetta Veglia

The rich and famous come to eat at Peter Graber's restaurant, then return to St. Moritz. Our inspector would prefer to stay in this old Engadine house; the only problem would be deciding which bedroom to choose. Each is named after the Swiss artist whose works decorate the walls. Two nudes by Gimmi are in room 5; once through the low doorway of room 1, the eye focuses on Giacomettis; but our inspector fell in love with room 8 and its Carigiet landscapes. Lying in bed, he enjoyed a roof-top view over the village to the mountains beyond. Furnishings provide a plain background to the art, but bathrooms are luxurious, with creamy marble, large mirrors, plenty of shelf space, whirlpool baths and separate lavatories.

The hotel and paintings belong to art dealer Fred Tschanz from Zurich. The cuisine and wine-list are the inspiration of Peter Graber, known for his *Stüvetta Klassiker*, beef marinated in hay and herbs for two days. Apart from oysters and lobster, the menu ranges from poached goose-liver, served with apple salad and fresh mango chutney, to cinnamon ice-cream with prunes soaked in *Pflümli*, plum schnapps. A romantic and gourmet hideaway.
Nearby winter sports; hiking.

7505 Celerina GR
Tel (081) 8338008
Fax (081) 8334542
Location in middle of village; ample car parking
Meals breakfast, lunch, dinner, snacks
Prices rooms SSS-SSSS with breakfast
Rooms 8 double; 1 suite; all have bath or shower, central heating, phone, TV, radio, minibar, safe
Facilities 3 dining-rooms; terrace
Credit cards AE, DC, MC, V
Children welcome but not suitable
Disabled not suitable
Pets accepted
Closed Nov to mid-Dec; after Easter to late June
Languages English, French, German, Italian
Managers Peter and Wera Graber

Graubünden

Davoserhof

'Chic and central' read the report on this hotel which is 'ideal for those who want to be close to all the facilities of this big, busy ski resort'. The Davoserhof already had a high reputation but 1993 saw extensive alterations. Bedrooms were enlarged and refurbished, using pale wood for built-in cupboards and desks. Bathrooms are first-rate: white marble with huge mirrors. Our inspector approved of the unusual fabrics which were selected by the owner, Mrs Petzold, rather than an interior decorator.

Downstairs, the Davoserstübli is the à la carte restaurant. With the old, caramel-coloured wood, carved chairs and *Kachelofen*, it has a pleasingly masculine look. More feminine is the honey-toned wood-panelling in the Jenatschstube. Paul Petzold loves his wines and has a lengthy list to complement the French-style cooking, from turbot in a salt crust to a tempting blood-orange charlotte with ginger-flavoured cream. Although the atmosphere seems luxurious and sedate, this is popular with families and the younger generation, who come for skiing and mountain-biking. In season, the bar has live music or a disco and stays open until 3 am. Happily, this is well-insulated from guests.

Nearby winter sports; hiking, lake.

Am Postplatz, 7270 Davos Platz GR
Tel (081) 4156666
Fax (081) 4156667
E-mail davoserhof@mirus.ch
Location in middle of Davos; own car parking, garage
Meals breakfast, lunch, dinner, snacks
Prices rooms S-SSS with breakfast
Rooms 17 double; 5 single; all have bath or shower, central heating, phone, TV, radio, minibar
Facilities 2 dining-rooms, 1 sitting-room, bar, terrace
Credit cards AE, MC, V
Children very welcome
Disabled some access
Pets not accepted
Closed never; restaurant only, Mon in summer
Languages English, French, German, Italian
Proprietors Petzold family

Graubünden

Haus Paradies

Serious food-lovers already know the name of this member of
Relais & Châteaux, thanks to the cooking of Austrian-born chef
Eduard Hitzbergen, who has gone from strength to strength,
achieving two well-deserved Michelin stars. His summer menu
included terrine of lobster with buck-wheat *blinis*, souffléd salmon
with basil sauce and duck breast glazed with honey and sesame
seeds, and partnered by potato dumplings. He buys lamb and
cheeses from locals, organic produce when possible and makes
his own bread, jam, ice cream, chocolates and pastry. Salads and
herbs come from the garden.

'We have a more relaxed, less formal style,' explained his wife,
Waltraud, as she arranged a table setting of delicate glasses and
polished silver, offset by a vase of wild flowers. 'Don't let the cubic-
look of the exterior put you off,' warned our inspector, who was
ready to unpack and stay for a month. Bedrooms and suites are
unashamedly modern, with the accent on comfort, perhaps with a
fireplace or ceramic oven: some have a Scandinavian look, others
Provençal-type patterns. All have a view across the valley to Tarasp
Castle and the Swiss Dolomites.

Nearby winter sports; hiking.

7551 Ftan GR
Tel (081) 8610808
Fax (081) 8610809
E-mail hotel.paradies@bluewin.ch
Location off small country
road, outside village; ample
car parking, garages
Meals breakfast, lunch,
dinner, snacks
Prices DB&B from SSS-SSSS
Rooms 9 double; 4 single; 8
suites; 1 family; all have bath
or shower, central heating,
phone, TV, radio, minibar.

Facilities 3 dining-rooms,
3 sitting-rooms, health spa;
terrace, garden
Credit cards AE, DC, MC, V
Children very welcome
Disabled not suitable
Pets accepted
Closed mid-Oct to mid-Dec;
after Easter to end May
Languages English, French,
German, Italian
Managers Waltraud and
Eduard Hitzberger

Graubünden

Meisser

Although Guarda has a population of only 140, it is a well-known tourist destination, thanks to its highly-decorated houses and resident craftsmen. Our inspector was relieved to have climbed the switchbacks from the valley by car, rather than the horse-drawn carriages that brought earlier visitors to this century-old inn. Built as a farmhouse in 1645, it was converted to an inn by Ralf Meisser's great-grandparents. Modern improvements have not always been sympathetic. The box-like restaurant extension has fabulous views over the Engadin Valley to the Swiss Dolomites but lacks the elegance of the old wood-panelled, high-ceilinged dining-room.

Bedrooms vary: in one, a handsome carved ceiling, in another, wallpaper that looks like a summer meadow, full of grasses and butterflies. Bathrooms are often problematical in conversions of old houses but there is no excuse for the linoleum floor and cheap, badly-hanging curtains which our reporter saw in one. He hoped that that was due for change in the continuing refurbishment programme. Despite these criticisms, he was impressed by the hospitality and carefully-prepared local dishes.

Nearby winter sports; hiking, tennis, golf, river-rafting.

7545 Guarda GR
Tel (081) 8622132
Fax (081) 8622480
E-mail meisser@mirus.ch
Location in heart of old mountain village; ample car parking
Meals breakfast, lunch, dinner, snacks
Prices rooms SS-SSS with breakfast; DB&B from SF135; meals from SF20
Rooms 14 double; 3 single; 5 suites; all have bath or shower, central heating, phone, minibar
Facilities 2 dining-rooms, 3 sitting-rooms; terrace, garden
Credit cards AE, DC, MC, V
Children welcome
Disabled not suitable
Pets accepted
Closed Nov to Whitsun
Languages English, French, German, Italian
Proprietors Meisser family

Graubünden

Chesa Grischuna

This has been a landmark in Klosters ever since it was built as the original railway hotel 60 years ago. Now it is just a few steps from the *Gotschnagrat-Parsenn* cable car and attracts outsiders all day long to the sunny terrace and the busy restaurant which serves up caviar and Châteaubriand as well as local specialities; in the afternoon, however, pastries are the draw for ladies waiting for husbands to finish skiing.

'Old-fashioned in the best sense' was the reaction to furnishings which aim for comfort rather than a designer look. Up the stairs that creak with age, bedrooms have double-thickness doors to ensure a quiet night's rest. The Chesa Grischuna happily manages to satisfy all types: the bar, is famous as an après-ski rendezvous, while upstairs the sitting room has games and cards, an open fireplace plus a mural detailing the history of Klosters and the Guler family. Hans Guler died in 1991 but his family continues the tradition of gracious hospitality. Their guest book reads like a Who's Who of statesmen and princes, actors and artists but everyone receives the same genuinely warm welcome. Important to book up well in advance.

Nearby winter sports; swimming, tennis.

7250 Klosters Platz GR
Tel (081) 4222222
Fax (081) 4222225
Location in the middle of town; car parking
Meals breakfast, lunch, dinner, snacks
Prices DB&B from SF110-340; meals from SF30
Rooms 18 double; 6 single; all have bath or shower, central heating, phone, TV, radio
Facilities dining-room, sitting-room, bar, bowling alley; terrace
Credit cards AE, DC, MC, V
Children welcome
Disabled not suitable
Pets accepted
Closed 6 weeks after Easter
Languages English, French, German, Italian
Proprietors Guler family

Graubünden

Walserhof

Beat Bolliger is one of Switzerland's finest chefs, stuffing ravioli with lobster or shrimps into courgette flowers or serving two mustard sauces and wild mushroom lasagna with roast guinea fowl. Other dishes are disarmingly simple: veal with herbs and *Rösti*, or pork with prunes and polenta. He also modernises local Prättigau dishes and boasts an array of 40 cheeses and four home-made breads. His wife Gabi, runs the pretty restaurant where white damask table-cloths, flowers and china stand out against the 300-year-old wood-panelling and beams, saved from a farmhouse.

Although the hotel is on the main road, bedrooms overlook hillside meadows. Gabi's attention to detail downstairs is repeated upstairs, where our female inspector approved of the Tréca adjustable beds and the careful mixing and toning of English fabrics for curtains, wall coverings and bedspreads. Colours are generally subdued: pine-green (number 14) or Monet-like blue and pink (number 15). She was also impressed by the bathrooms with *café au lait* marble, film-star mirrors and double wash-basins. Large cupboards are good for families on winter holidays and the ski-school is only a minute away.

Nearby winter sports; tennis, golf, mountain-biking.

7250 Klosters Platz GR
Tel (081) 4102929
Fax (081) 4102939
Location on main road on edge of village; ample car parking
Meals breakfast, lunch, dinner
Prices rooms SS-SSSS with breakfast
Rooms 11 double; 3 suites; all have bath or shower, central heating, phone, TV, radio, minibar

Facilities dining-room, sauna, lift/elevator
Credit cards AE, DC, MC, V
Children very welcome
Disabled reasonable access
Pets accepted
Closed late Oct to early Dec; mid-Apr to mid-Jun; restaurant only, Mon in May
Languages English, French, German, Italian
Managers Gabi and Beat Bolliger

Graubünden

Posta Veglia/Pöstli

Laax is one of the prettiest villages in the upper Rhine Valley and the Posta Veglia is arguably the region's prettiest inn. In 1978, Peter Panier gave up his marketing job in Zurich and came home, to create 'the kind of hotel that I always wanted to stay in'. The stone building with green shutters was once the hub of the community, encorporating schoolhouse, shop and *Stube*. Panier scoured antique shops for old furniture and pictures, stripped the paint off walls to reveal honey-coloured wood panelling, fired up the *Davetscherofen* and installed an old wind-up gramophone in the informal *Beizli* restaurant.

Upstairs, the old schoolroom is now the *Arvenstube*, complete with heart-backed chairs, deep red curtains and stern grandmas staring down from sepia photos. Food is traditional Swiss 'because people want that in the country but we have a lighter touch'. That does not mean tiny portions, however, whether it is fresh salmon or beef carbonnade; and there is always *Rösti*. Each bedroom looks different: swathes of gold fabric above the bed in one, painted *Bauern* furniture in another, a sleigh bed in a single and views of the mountains in the attic *Panoramazimmer*.

Nearby winter sports; river-rafting, walking, mountain-biking.

7031 Laax GR
Tel (081) 9214466
Fax (081) 9213400
Location in heart of village; ample car parking
Meals breakfast, lunch, dinner, snacks
Prices rooms SS-SSSS with breakfast
Rooms 6 double; all have bath or shower, central heating, phone, TV, radio
Facilities 3 dining-rooms, bar; terrace, garden

Credit cards MC, V
Children welcome but not suitable
Disabled not suitable
Pets accepted
Closed Nov to mid-Dec; after Easter to July
Languages English, French, German, Italian
Proprietor Peter Panier

Graubünden

Seehof

Folk architecture is such a Swiss tradition that a brand-new hotel poses a challenge to interior designers. The phoenix that rose in 1992 from the ashes of the old Seehof at the Valbella end of the lake is a tribute to the imagination of the first manager Wisy Kempf. Mirrors add light to corridors and every white wall bears a striking modern painting that deserves a second look. Valuable hand-woven Persian nomad carpets in warm, rust-red colours are spread over the grey-green granite floors and soften the strong contemporary line.

Since May 1998, Jürg Roschein and his wife Christine have given a new impetus to an already enthusiastic staff. German-born Rolf Mauch is a health-conscious chef who works with fresh, seasonal produce, and the pale pink and pine restaurant is the focal point of a visit. More familiar dishes, however, such as spaghetti and steak, snails on toast and trout *meunière* are also on the menu. Bedrooms are large, with furnishings of pale lilac or blue against white walls; all have lake views. Family-friendly and cheerful, the Seehof is popular with active types who like the great outdoors and want an active holiday.

Nearby winter sports; golf, sailing, tennis, walking, windsurfing.

7077 Valbella-Lenzerheide GR
Tel (081) 3843535
Fax (071) 7874284
E-mail hotel@seehof-valbella.ch
Location by lake, away from main road; ample car parking
Meals breakfast, lunch, dinner, snacks
Prices rooms SS-SSSS with breakfast
Rooms 25 double; 1 suite; all have bath or shower, central heating, phone, TV, radio; some minibar
Facilities 3 dining-rooms, bar, sauna and fitness area, lift/elevator; terrace, garden
Credit cards AE, DC, MC, V
Children very welcome
Disabled reasonable access
Pets accepted
Closed never
Languages English, French, German, Italian
Managers Raschein family

Graubünden

Guarda Val

'Luxury in the farmyard, cows and *haute cuisine* – you have to see it to believe it' read the report on this four-star hotel in the middle of the *Maiensäss*, the May pastures above Lenzerheide. Abandoned 50 years ago, these stone and wood buildings stood empty until the late 1960s when a Zurich businessman converted them, creating a country inn that is one-of-a-kind. Even the farmers came back. Now ErichKurzen is the owner and he has redecorated bedrooms with flair, using pale colours and pear wood, and revamped bathrooms.

'Regulars come three or four times a year, treat it like their country home and expect to have "their" room.' That could be number 47, high under the roof with tiny windows; or *Stailetta*, the split-level studio suite straight out of a design magazine with a huge bathroom fit for a Hollywood star. The main building dates from 1810 but looks medieval, with a gallery in the gourmet restaurant. In a former cowshed the informal Crap Naros restaurant serves local dishes such as venison with red cabbage. In winter, guests who ski out and ski back store their equipment in a ski room which, in summer, is the dairy.

Nearby downhill, cross-country skiing; tennis, golf, sailing.

7078 Lenzerheide/Sporz GR
Tel (081) 3858585
Fax (081) 3858595
Location in meadows on hillside above Lenzerheide; ample car parking
Meals breakfast, lunch, dinner, snacks
Prices rooms SS-SSSS with breakfast
Rooms 20 double; 14 suites; all have bath or shower, central heating, phone, TV, radio, minibar, hairdrier, safe

Facilities 2 dining-rooms, sitting-room, bar, sauna and fitness area; terrace, garden
Credit cards AE, DC, MC, V
Children very welcome
Disabled not suitable
Pets accepted
Closed Nov to mid-Dec; after Easter to mid-June
Languages English, French, German, Italian
Proprietor Erich Kurzen

Graubünden

❈ Village inn, Madulain ❈

Stüva Colani

'I'm from near Paris, a little place called Fontainebleau – have you heard of it?' joked Gilbert Stöhr as we looked round his hotel. Although the building is 200 years old, much of the interior is modern and open-plan. Take the Tavolino, the informal restaurant topped by pyramid-like skylights and brightened by a huge mural of people, some of whom, we suspect, are among the 130-strong population of Madulain. Perfect for families, the pasta menu includes *Maccheroni alla mafiosa* (with aubergines and chili peppers). The gourmet restaurant, however, is aimed at adults. In the old alcoves where meat once hung for smoking, soft lighting flickers on the white walls and pinky-brown leather banquettes. 'I look for contrasts in food,' explains Gilbert, whose menus include salmon tartare with blinis, pigeon stuffed with *ris de veau* and ravioli with chives.

We liked the blend of old and new, the slate floors and furnishings in gentle blues and greys, with rose pink for warmth. Bedrooms vary in size but number 17, right at the top, is a family room, with plenty of space for clothes and suitcases. It would be easy to become a regular visitor to this delightful inn.

Nearby St. Moritz; National Park; fishing, hiking, winter sports.

7523 Madulain GR	sitting-room, bar; terrace,
Tel (081) 8541771	garden
Fax (081) 8541485	**Credit cards** MC, V
Location in middle of village;	**Children** welcome
ample car parking	**Disabled** not suitable
Meals breakfast, lunch,	**Pets** not accepted
dinner, snacks	**Closed** Nov to mid-Dec; after
Prices rooms S-SS with	Easter to early June;
breakfast	restaurant only, Wed, Thurs
Rooms 14 double; 1 single;	lunch in low season
1 family; all have bath or	**Languages** English, French,
shower, central heating,	German, Italian
phone, radio, TV by request	**Proprietors** Stöhr family
Facilities 3 dining-rooms,	

Graubünden

Village inn, Malans

Weisskreuz

Our inspectors are rarely taken by surprise but they scribbled enthusiastically from the moment they climbed the stairs of this old inn. The Bündnerstuben, two formal dining rooms, are 'lovely examples of old wood panelling, chandeliers, antique furniture, fresh flowers and baroque clocks'. Far below, a giant wine-press in the Zum Torkel is 'the wine-making equivalent of the dinosaur, enormous, a magnificent relic of a bygone era'. In the surrounding Bündner Herrschaft vineyards, a new generation of wine makers is impressing oenophiles with Chardonnays as well as traditional Blauburgunder and Riesling-Sylvaner grapes.

With its rustic wooden furniture, the Malanserstube is the meeting point for locals who are fans of the chef's so-called 'slow food'. Using fresh, seasonal and regional produce, he cooks traditional *Bündnce* dishes such as *Capuns* (sausage wrapped in chard) or *pizokels* (buck-wheat pasta).

Bedrooms are ultra-modern, with unusual locker-like cupboards, Italian lighting and photographs of architectural details such as gargoyles on butter-yellow walls. Bathrooms are first-rate. Disabled guests are well catered for.

Nearby vineyards, wine villages of Bündner Herrschaft.

7208 Malans GR
Tel (081) 3228161
Fax (081) 3228162
E-mail gtinguely@weisskreuz.com
Location in middle of village; ample car parking
Meals breakfast, lunch, dinner, snacks
Prices rooms SS-SSS with breakfast
Rooms 11 double; all have shower, central heating, phone, TV, radio, minibar
Facilities 5 dining-rooms, bar, lift/elevator; terrace
Credit cards AE, MC, V
Children welcome
Disabled 4 special rooms
Pets accepted
Closed never
Languages English, French, German, Italian
Manager Gabriel Tinguely

Graubünden

Albana

When Andreas and Regula Ludwig took over in 1996, they followed a manager and chef who had built up a fine reputation for this stylish and contemporary hotel, just a short drive from St. Moritz. But readers' reports about the new team are favourable, with particular praise for the new spa facilities. "Our guests are more interested in well-being, than fitness, so the gymnasium has been changed to offer physiotherapy and acupuncture," Andreas Ludwig told us.

The bedrooms, however, remain bright and practical, with local *Arvenholz* (larch), blue or pink fabrics, crisp white duvets and equally spotless bathrooms. The informal Spunta and the wood-panelled Gourmet restaurant are the province of a new Swiss chef, who adds a Mediterranean twist to his modern cooking, which has caught the attention of food critics. As for the guests, they enjoy the good life, with a little sport for variety. Once a week, Andreas maintains a laudable Swiss hoteliers' tradition by taking his guests up into the mountains. In winter, they go skiing before stopping at a hut for raclette or fondue. In summer, a picnic makes a hike doubly enjoyable.

Nearby hiking, mountain-biking; winter sports.

7513 Silvaplana GR
Tel (081) 8289292
Fax (081)8288181
Location in middle of village; ample car parking
Meals breakfast, lunch, dinner, snacks
Prices rooms SF115-320 with breakfast; DB&B from SF175; reduction for children; meals from SF50
Rooms 25 double; 10 single; all have bath or shower, central heating, phone, TV, radio, minibar, hairdrier, safe
Facilities 2 dining-rooms, sitting-room, bar, sauna, fitness area, lift/elevator; terrace, garden
Credit cards AE, DC, MC, V
Children welcome
Disabled some access
Pets accepted
Closed after Easter to July
Languages English, French, German, Italian
Proprietors Regula and Andreas Ludwig

Graubünden

Schlosshotel Chastè

'Yet another pretty village, yet another hotel with a fascinating history' wrote our inspector at the start of a lengthy description. The building dates back over 500 years and the *Stüva* still has its tiny trapdoor, through which the farmer's family would squeeze to get to the sleeping quarters above. Rudolf Pazeller's grandfather started the *Stüvetta* in 1912 to cater for workers restoring the castle and despite subsequent expansion, the overall look is traditional. Decorative carving is everywhere, floors are of glazed terracotta cobbles, and the old kitchen could be a museum. In total contrast are the modern exercise equipment and sauna down below that were cut out of the granite mountain.

The hotel is full of suprises: gardens and terraces on different levels, fragrant with herbs and ablaze with flowers, even a pavilion where the famous local mineral water is on tap, like beer. As for bedrooms, sit back in the bath of number 124 and stare straight at the castle; lean on the balcony of number 119 and imagine it full of hay when this was the barn. Our reporter admired the four-poster beds and carved ceilings but could do without the burgundy-coloured wallpaper in number 120.

Nearby Tarasp Castle; Swiss National Park; winter sports.

7553 Tarasp-Sparsels GR
Tel (081) 8641775
Fax (081) 8649970
E-mail chaste@bluewin.ch
Location in heart of old village; car parking nearby
Meals breakfast, lunch, dinner, snacks
Prices DB&B from SS-SSSS;
Rooms 17 double; 2 single; 1 suite; all have bath or shower, central heating, phone, TV, radio, minibar, hairdrier, safe; some non-smoking

Facilities 2 dining-rooms, sitting-room, bar, sauna and fitness area; terrace, garden
Credit cards not accepted
Children very welcome
Disabled not suitable
Pets accepted
Closed Nov to mid-Dec; Easter to 2nd May
Languages English, French, German, Italian
Proprietors Pazeller family

Valais

❋ Mountain inn, Champex-Lac ❋

Belvédère

Walk past the stuffed marmot on the stone terrace, duck into the
low-ceilinged bar, and smells of country cooking assault the
nostrils at almost any time of day. This inn is unashamedly
informal and decidedly quirky. Puppets and violins hang from the
ceiling, working firearms adorn the walls of the bar. The sitting-
room has a lived-in look no decorator could hope to achieve, with
books, binoculars plus Gabriel Favre's prize cow bell and his
wife Irène's crocheted doilies adorning the authentically-ageing
peasant-style furnishings. Fighting cows, called Queens, are
unique to this region; mine host owns several and has a video to
explain it all.

The narrow upstairs corridors and ceilings are lined with a local
red pine, some of which has been replaced recently with discon-
certingly fresh wood, albeit in the the traditional style. Lace pil-
lows and hand-painted bedboards evoke the mountain world of
another century. This inn has acquired a cult status among culti-
vated folk from Geneva, who ignore the green linoleum floor in
the dining-room and the small bathrooms, and enjoy what is a
successful blend of kitsch and basic comforts.

Nearby tennis, swimming, walking; winter sports.

1938 Champex-Lac VS
Tel (027) 7831114
Fax (027) 7832576
Location in woods at edge of
lakeside village; ample car
parking
Meals breakfast, lunch,
dinner, snacks
Prices rooms SS with
breakfast
Rooms 4 double; 1 single;
3 family; all have bath or
shower, central heating, TV,
hairdrier

Facilities dining-room, sitting-
room, bar; terrace, garden
Credit cards MC, V
Children welcome
Disabled not suitable
Pets accepted
Closed early Dec
Languages English, French,
German, Italian
Proprietors Gabriel and Irène
Favre

Valais

❋ **Mountain-resort hotel, Crans-Montana** ❋

Le Mont-Blanc

Emerging fresh and smiling from his kitchen, dressed in the pristine white of a chef, Jean-Pierre Gasser is the embodiment of Swiss hospitality. In his opinion, the customer is king. He does not believe in having 'environmentally friendly' signs advising guests not to waste water or use too many towels. As for his cuisine, that is classic yet light, the kind you can eat three times a day with relish and still not get fat. The wine-list features local Valais names like Dôle and Fendant, rounded out with superb Bordeaux and Burgundy vintages.

The Mont-Blanc has the biggest terrace and the best view in Crans-Montana, offering a retreat well away from the bustle of busy downtown Crans itself, crammed with Rolls Royces and Gucci shoppers. All rooms face south, enjoying a view of the Rhône Valley, described as one of the best anywhere in the Alps. Bedrooms are to be upgraded in 1994 to provide greater comfort but our inspector hopes the 1950s radio sets will remain. Downstairs, the restaurant's circular fireplace is large enough to roast a VW 'Beatle' in, while flowers in huge copper pots hang from rafters. Outside, a basketball hoop awaits the energetic.
Nearby walking; winter sports.

3963 Crans-Montana, Les Plans Mayens VS
Tel (027) 4813143
Fax (027) 4813146
Location above resort; ample car parking
Meals breakfast, lunch, dinner, snacks
Prices rooms S-SSS with breakfast
Rooms 10 double; 3 suites; all have bath or shower, central heating, phone, radio; some TV

Facilities dining-room, sitting-room, bar, TV room; terrace, garden
Credit cards AE, DC, MC, V
Children welcome
Disabled not suitable
Pets accepted
Closed mid-Oct to mid-Dec; end April to early June
Languages English, French, German, Italian
Proprietor Jean-Pierre Gasser

Valais

✳ **Spa hotel, Leukerbad / Loèche-les-Bains** ✳

Les Sources des Alpes

'This is the Swiss hotel of my dreams,' headlined the report of our inspector, a former foreign correspondent who has travelled the world. From the red carpet stretching up the glass-canopied entrance, to the heated towels at the thermal-spring fed swimming-pool, the luxury is always discreet and unobtrusive. Leukerbad is both a ski resort and a health spa, and some of the treatments at the hotel are complicated enough to require the in-house doctor. Most guests, however, come to be cosseted and to treat themselves to chef Peter Schetter's delicious but low-calorie *cuisine du marché'* which emphasizes the fresh local produce from the valley of the Rhône.

Bedrooms, most of which would be called suites elsewhere, are named after flowers, fruits, wines or even flavours, such as Vanilla or Honey. Each is furnished individually in restful colours but all have bouquets of alpine flowers, bathrobes and slippers as well as notepaper embossed with the guest's name. The fitness and indoor swimming-pool area is infused with herbal aromas, while the garden is an oasis of tranquillity that is as effective a cure for stress as any of the more exotic spa therapies.

Nearby hiking; thermal baths; winter sports.

3954 Leukerbad VS
Tel (027) 4705751
Fax (027) 4703533
E-mail sda.leukerbad@spectraweb.ch
Location in spa; ample underground car parking
Meals breakfast, lunch, dinner, snacks
Prices rooms SSSS with breakfast
Rooms 30 double; all have bath or shower, central heating, phone, TV, radio, minibar, hairdrier

Facilities dining-room, sitting-room, bar, sauna, fitness area, lift/elevator; terrace, garden, indoor and outdoor swimming-pools, spa treatments
Credit cards AE, DC, MC, V
Children welcome
Disabled not suitable
Pets accepted
Closed never
Languages English, French, German, Italian, Spanish
Manager Andreas Stump

Valais

Aux Mille Etoiles

Ingrid and Hansruedi Berner-Mol have taken over the hotel from their parents, Elly and Jan. Now the third generation are also involved in what is a real family-oriented hotel. Spacious and regularly redecorated, this has all the atmosphere of a chalet.

The main sitting-room looks on to the indoor swimming-pool, which itself opens out into the garden. As for accommodation, choose from junior suites like number 44 which is open-plan and airy, with white pine and contemporary fabrics, an extra-large bathroom and a balcony looking over the rugged Trient valley. The family rooms include a separate room for children, with bunk-beds and full bathroom facilities; and there are also smaller bedrooms which have not yet been renovated and are consequently cheaper.

A former journalist, Jan Mol, publishes a daily newsletter with a weather report and suggestions for hikes or ski trips. Convivial *raclette* evenings every Wednesday are the only threat to an otherwise pervasive mountain calm. The ski-fields above the hotel are the only spot in Valais where the Matterhorn and Mont Blanc are visible at the same time.

Nearby zoo, car museum, lakes; winter sports.

1923 Les Marécottes VS
Tel (027) 7611666
Fax (027) 7611600
Location at top of village; ample car parking
Meals breakfast, lunch, dinner, snacks
Prices rooms S-SS with breakfast; meals from SF18
Rooms 15 double; 4 single; 4 suites; 2 family; all have bath or shower, central heating, phone, radio; TV, minibar, hairdrier

Facilities 2 dining-rooms, 2 sitting-rooms, bar, sauna, fitness area, lift/elevator, indoor swimming-pool, games room; terrace, garden
Credit cards MC, V
Children very welcome
Disabled not suitable
Pets accepted
Closed Nov to mid-Dec; 4 weeks after Easter
Languages English, French, German, Dutch
Proprietors Berner-Mol family

Valais

Golf Hotel

'This is the oldest hotel in town, the one with the most character,' according to our inspector, who added that the owner, Jacky Bessard, is a golf fan. He regularly plays with guests on the 18-hole course on the high meadows, having given up para-gliding. Always ready with advice on where to walk, he also organises a weekly cook-out in the mountains.

In a resort full of the dedicated followers of fashion, this inn is happy to look out-of-date, with armchairs and carpets in good condition but 'of another era'. Bedrooms have floral wallpaper matched by fresh flowers in vases and in boxes on the large, communal balconies. As for views, what else but the Grand Combin, Mont Blanc and the Trient? Downstairs, the piano bar is civilised, with squashy leather sofas and music soft enough to allow conversation; a world away from the disco scene for which Verbier is famous. Traditional French cooking in the restaurant provides welcome relief from a diet of fondue and *raclette*. The large garden has a wall of willows to block out the noise of traffic on the main road which, happily, ceases at nightfall so guests can enjoy a good night's sleep.

Nearby winter sports.

1936 Verbier VS
Tel (027) 7716515
Fax (027) 7711488
E-mail golfotel@axiom.ch
Location in middle of town; ample car parking
Meals breakfast, lunch, dinner, snacks
Prices rooms SS-SSS with breakfast
Rooms 30 double; all have bath or shower, central heating, phone, TV, radio
Facilities dining-room, 2 sitting-rooms, bar, sauna and fitness area, lift/elevator, TV room; terrace, garden
Credit cards AE, MC, V
Children welcome
Disabled not suitable
Pets accepted
Closed Oct-Nov; May-June
Languages English, French, German, Italian
Proprietor Jacky Bessard

Valais

❅ Mountain resort hotel, Verbier ❅

Rosalp

Roland Pierroz is a star. No one has done more to raise the culinary consciousness of Valais out of the fondue pot and up to the level of the best French restaurants. His parents ran the hotel for 30 years and now he is rated one of the top six chefs in the country. Everything in the restaurant and hotel reflects his personal taste, particularly the original artwork on the walls. There are two restaurants, the Pierroz and La Pinte; the latter is the more affordable. His 35,000-bottle wine cellar with computer controlled temperature is open to visits, often conducted by the rotund, bearded chef himself.

A member of the Relais & Chateaux group, standards of comfort here are high. Some bedrooms are furnished in city chic, with lots of polished glass and brass and shiny, impressionistic fabrics covering walls and beds. Number 315 opens on to a large terrace with flowers and a view of the Grand Combin; number 344, an impressive suite with a wrap-around balcony, has a stone fireplace plus a full kitchen artfully concealed behind antique, leaded mirrors. A few are cosy and completely wood-panelled but this is no rural retreat; it is right in the heart of Verbier.

Nearby winter sports; golf, tennis, swimming-pool, walking.

1936 Verbier
Tel (027) 7716323
Fax (027) 7711059
Location near the Place Centrale; own car parking, some covered
Meals breakfast, lunch, dinner, snacks
Prices rooms SS-SSSS with breakfast
Rooms 17 double; 1 single; 3 suites; all have bath or shower, central heating, phone, TV, radio, minibar, hairdrier
Facilities 2 dining-rooms, sitting-room, bar, TV room, sauna, fitness area, lift/elevator; terrace
Credit cards AE, DC, MC, V
Children welcome
Disabled not suitable
Pets accepted
Closed Oct-Nov; May-June
Languages English, French, German, Italian
Proprietor Roland Pierroz

Valais

❋ **Mountain resort hotel, Zermatt** ❋

Alex Schlosshotel Tenne

Not really a castle, the Schlosshotel is half old wooden chalet, half new stonework; inside, 'eclectic' was the description of furnishings which, for example, combined Flemish-style paintings on yellow embossed wallpaper with Byzantine icons. The oldest part of the building, dating back 150 years, is now the barn-like restaurant. Except for the nude wooden figure suspended from the rafters, this looks like hundreds of other fondue and *raclette* places all over Valais. Here, however, such cheese dishes are not served, although meat fondues are.

All south-facing bedrooms have large balconies with views of the Matterhorn. Some are decorated in what the Perrens call 'rustic' style, others feature vaulted ceilings with stained-glass skylights and white wicker furniture. There is a jacuzzi in each of the commodious bathrooms, and the hotel boasts a first-rate health spa with sauna.

Being in the middle of Zermatt, the hotel cannot guarantee total silence. It is, however, right next to the Gornergrat train station, a boon for skiers who would otherwise have to take electric taxis to lift stations.

Nearby indoor tennis; walking; winter sports.

3920 Zermatt VS
Tel (027) 9671801
Fax (027) 9671803
E-mail tenne.zermatt@reconline.ch
Location next to Gornergrat train station; cars must be left at station in Täsch
Meals breakfast, lunch, dinner, snacks
Prices DB&B from SS-SSSS
Rooms 25 double; 5 single; 5 suites; all have bath or shower, central heating, phone, TV, radio, jacuzzi; some minibar
Facilities dining-room, sitting-room, bar, sauna and fitness area, lift/elevator; terrace, garden
Credit cards AE, MC, V
Children welcome
Disabled not suitable
Pets accepted
Closed Oct, Nov
Languages English, French, German, Italian, Spanish
Proprietors Sonja and Christina Perren

Valais

❄ Mountain resort hotel, Zermatt ❄

Romantikhotel Julen

For over 70 years the Julen has been a fixture in this car-free village, famous for its winter sports, but equally attractive in summer for hiking, climbing and summer skiing. Whatever the season, views of the Matterhorn are breathtaking. Julen is a common name in Zermatt, where Paul and Daniela Julen gave their hotel a complete facelift in 1997 and 1998. First, they added a futuristic 3-storey pool and relaxation centre with a so-called 'adventure swimming pool', gymnasium and sauna. Then they knocked through some walls to create more spacious bedrooms, upgrading the comfort levels throughout.

This is still very much a family hotel. As well as the three young Julens, many guests remember Bobi, the friendly working sheep-dog. Now a new dog, Miss, fills that role. Thankfully, some things never change. On winter evenings, everyone still makes for the *Schäferstübli* (sheep room), with its sheepskin-covered chairs and huge, horned mountain sheep heads adorning the walls. The restaurant, with its Valais specialities, has always had a good reputation. Apart from the obvious fondues and raclettes, the lamb dishes are a highlight.

Nearby winter sports; walking, the Matterhorn

3920 Zermatt VS
Tel (027) 966 7600
Fax (027) 966 7676
E-mail hotel.julen@zermatt.ch
Location on edge of village; cars must be left at station in Täsch
Meals breakfast, lunch, dinner, snacks
Prices rooms from SSS-SSSS dinner, bed and breakfast
Rooms 25 double; 3 single; 5 suite; all have telephone, TV, radio, hairdrier, minibar, safe, balcony
Facilities 2 dining-rooms, sitting-room, bar, lift/elevator, indoor swimming-pool and health complex; terrace, garden
Credit cards AE, DC, MC, V
Children very welcome
Disabled not suitable
Pets accepted **Closed** never
Languages English, French, German,
Proprietors Daniela and Paul Julen

Ticino

Restaurant with rooms, Carnago-Origlio

Deserto

'A traditional grotto restaurant, with stone walls, tiled floors and old beams festooned with garlic and hams' read the report on the 100-year-old Deserto. Since 1937, the Testoni family have been grilling at the open fireplace where wood, charcoal and an armful of kebab skewers stand ready for use. Our inspector was impressed by the waiter, who enthusiastically explained the menu of local specialities to diners in four different languages. She decided on risotto with *porcini* mushrooms, rabbit with pistachios and fresh berries for dessert. The wine-list is a delight, offering one of the most comprehensive lists of local Merlot wines, which are stored below in the deep cellars.

Now those who want to stay put after dinner can climb the stairs to the newly-refurbished bedrooms. With plain wooden beds and floral duvet covers, these continue the country look of the restaurant but bathrooms are modern and mattresses firm. Number 25 has a small terrace, while number 13 has steep steps leading to a balcony with an extra bed for children. Beyond the vine-covered terrace at the back is a small play area. Although right on the road, traffic noise does not intrude.

Nearby Capriasca Valley; riding, golf, skiing, tennis, walking.

6945 Carnago-Origlio TI
Tel (091) 9451216
Fax (091) 9455072
Location in village, 15 minutes' drive north of Lugano; ample car parking
Meals breakfast, lunch, dinner, snacks
Prices rooms S-SS with breakfast
Rooms 12 double; all have bath or shower, central heating, phone, TV, radio, minibar, hairdrier, safe

Facilities dining-room, sitting-room, bar; terrace, garden
Credit cards AE, DC, MC, V
Children welcome
Disabled not suitable
Pets accepted
Closed never
Languages English, French, German, Italian
Proprietors Testoni family

Ticino

Holiday hotel, Locarno at Orselina

Hotel Mirafiori

High above Lake Maggiore, Orselina was known for its healthy climate which gave relief to patients suffering from chest ailments. Nowadays, this hill village is one of many on the 'tour' of the Locarno area. At first glance, the Mirafiori looks like many other hotels in the Ticino region. What makes it special, however, is the unaffected warmth of the welcome. Rooms are named for local flora and fauna such as *Lucciola* (firefly) and *Cigno* (swan) but not all are in the main building. Some are in small annexes up the terraced hillside at the back. *Formica* (ant), for instance, is large, with a floor-to-ceiling window and its own covered terrace, while *Margherita* (daisy) is a little 'Hansel and Gretel' cottage, all on its own and a favourite with newlyweds. The garden, full of honeysuckle and beds of lilies, has the swimming-pool plus a miniature picnic table for young children a few steps from the adult-sized version.

Since 1952, the Schmid family has been in charge. Now son Carlo is the chef and his cooking obviously hits the spot. 'Excellent food here,' our inspector was told by an English guest who savoured the Ticinese specialities as well as international dishes.

Nearby Basilica of Madonna del Sasso; golf, tennis, walking.

6644 Locarno-Orselina, Via Al Parco TI
Tel (091) 7431877
Fax (091) 7437739
Location in Orselina, high on hillside; ample car parking, some under cover
Meals breakfast, lunch, dinner, snacks
Prices rooms SS-SSS with breakfast
Rooms 25 double; all have bath or shower, central heating, phone, TV, radio

Facilities dining-room, sitting-room, bar, sauna, Jacuzzi, lift/elevator; terrace, garden, swimming-pool, table-tennis
Credit cards AE, DC, MC, V
Children very welcome
Disabled not suitable
Pets accepted but not in garden or restaurant
Closed early Nov to mid-March
Languages English, French, German, Italian
Proprietors Schmid family

Ticino

Luxury villa, Lugano

Villa Principe Leopoldo

'Above it all, literally and figuratively' was our inspector's reaction to this former holiday home of Leopold of Hapsburg which offers 'a prince's seclusion and a prince's view' of Lugano, ferries criss-crossing the lake and Mont Brè and Monte San Salvatore. On the curved terrace, colour is provided by lavender and azaleas, the perfume by jasmine, which climbs the 14 columns and hangs from the long balcony above.

A hotel only since 1985, the original building has been preserved, with parquet floors, heavy chandeliers and trompe-l'oeil paintings. The hillside under the terrace was dug away to build the bedrooms. All are junior suites, with picture windows, walk-in closets, electronic shutters, huge mirrors and furnishings of green or pink with gold creating a rich but uncluttered look. 'Dramatic' was the verdict on the lemon-print fabric and black rattan chairs of the breakfast-room, which looks out on the fan-shaped swimming-pool. Everywhere are portraits of nobility, busts of Roman emperors and English sporting prints. The restaurant serves imaginative Italian dishes as well as caviar and lobster. 'This is luxury without overwhelming formality.'

Nearby lake, Lugano; casino, golf, riding, tennis, windsurfing.

6900 Lugano, Via Montalbano 5, TI
Tel (091) 9858855
Fax (091) 9858825
E-mail info@leopoldo.ch
Location high on Collina d'Oro; ample car parking, garage
Meals breakfast, lunch, dinner, snacks
Prices rooms SSSS with breakfast
Rooms 37 suites; all have bath and shower, central heating,

phone, TV, radio, minibar, hairdrier, safe
Facilities 2 dining-rooms, 2 sitting-rooms, bar, sauna and fitness area, lift/elevator; 2 terraces, garden, swimming-pool **Credit cards** AE, DC, MC, V **Children** welcome
Disabled not suitable
Pets accepted
Closed never
Languages English, French, German, Italian
Manager Maurice Ursch

Ticino

City hotel, Lugano

Romantik Hotel Ticino

It is hard to imagine a small, quiet place to stay right in the heart of Lugano, but this is it. Owner Claire Buchmann set out to create a meeting place for artists and intellectuals but anyone can enjoy this 400-year-old palazzo. On the edge of the Piazza Cioccaro, in the maze-like central pedestrianised area, the entrance is hidden behind a wrought-iron gate hung with vines. 'Art and gastronomy' is the Buchmann's motto and the plain linen, mahogany and green leather banquettes of the vaulted restaurant on the ground floor provide a subdued background for fine food matched by the fine paintings on the walls.

Upstairs, three tiers of arcades overlook a small courtyard, which, with its plants and tinkling fountains, is a soothing haven from the city. Bedrooms come in different sizes and shapes; some have plain walls, others delicate floral wallpaper but all have first-rate beds. 'I have a back problem, so I know how important a good mattress is,' Mrs. Buchmann told us. In an old building like this, bathrooms are going to be small but these are well laid-out, with adequate shelf space. A cosy library and tiny bar complete this discrete little gem.

Nearby old town, lake, parks; golf, tennis, riding, windsurfing.

6901 Lugano, Piazza Cioccaro 1 TI
Tel (091) 9227772
Fax (091) 9236278
Location in heart of old town, garage available
Meals breakfast, lunch, dinner, snacks
Prices rooms SSS-SSSS with breakfast
Rooms 14 double; 2 single; 4 suites; all have bath or shower, central heating, phone, radio, minibar, hairdrier; some non-smoking rooms
Facilities dining room, sitting-room, bar, lift/elevator; terrace, garden
Credit cards AE, MC, V
Children welcome
Disabled not suitable
Pets accepted
Closed early Jan to mid-Feb
Languages English, French, German, Italian
Proprietors Claire and Samuel Buchmann

Ticino

Villa Margherita

Once in a while we feel justified in including a hotel with more than 30 rooms. Having started by renovating a simple pension 40 years ago, the Herzog family have expanded gradually by buying nearby houses in the hills behind Lugano. With only a few rooms in each of the six villas, the ambience remains 'small' and more 'Relais' than 'Châteaux', thanks to furnishings that are less plush than many other members of that hotel group. 'Everything has a story,' we were told, as we noted the framed African batik and tie-dyed Chinese fabric, the paintings and statues, many collected by Kurt Herzog during his career as an international airline pilot.

His love of plants is evident, with potted orchids and cactus as well as landscaped terraces, an expanse of lawn flat enough for croquet and even a small vineyard. Choose between the indoor, salt-water plunge pool or the outdoor swimming-pool, then take afternoon tea on the large, covered terrace before retiring to the garden pavilion, the games room, or one of the many private corners to read before sitting down to a five-course dinner. Bedrooms vary from the simple to the very comfortable, often with a Scandinavian look.

Nearby lake, Lugano; golf, riding, tennis, windsurfing.

6935 Bosco Luganese, TI
Tel (091) 6115111
Fax (091) 6115110
E-mail margherita@relaischateaux.fr
Location above Bioggio; ample car parking, garages
Meals breakfast, lunch, dinner, snacks
Prices rooms SS-SSSS with breakfast
Rooms 34 double; 2 single; 2 suites; all have bath or shower, phone, TV, radio, minibar, hairdrier, safe

Facilities 2 dining-rooms, 3 sitting-rooms, bar, indoor heated plunge pool, lift/elevator; terrace, garden, 2 swimming-pools
Credit cards AE, DC, MC, V
Children welcome
Disabled not suitable
Pets accepted
Closed Nov to Easter
Languages English, French, German, Italian
Proprietors Herzog family

Ticino

Old villa, Lugano at Caslano

Albergo Gardenia

This is where we would go to escape the stress of modern life. The appeal of this 150-year-old summer villa is the sense of seclusion, perhaps a throwback to the convent which once stood on the site. Throughout, old beams and exposed brickwork contrast with the owner's private collection of contemporary Swiss paintings and sculpture.

Brigitte Piazzoli runs the hotel with her husband, Silvano, whose menus of French and Italian classics have made a name for the small Bacco restaurant. Our breakfast was one of the best we had in Switzerland: truly fresh orange juice, delicious breads, cut-your-own cheese, and a fruit salad full of strawberries. In the main house, four 'panorama' rooms on the top floor boast conservatories. All bedrooms are large, with chic Italian furniture and unusual colour schemes such as plum and grey or mango and dark gold; but beware the nightmare inducing Franz Falch painting in number 36. Rooms in the Casa Azzurra annexe are smaller but have private patios for sunbathing and direct access to the garden, full of potted gardenias and shaded by two enormous paulownia trees.

Nearby lake, Lugano; golf, riding, tennis, walking.

6987 Caslano-Lugano TI
Tel (091) 6061716
Fax (091) 6062642
E-mail albergo-gardenia@bluewin.ch
Location on hillside, edge of village; ample car parking
Meals breakfast, lunch, dinner, snacks
Prices DB&B from SS-SSS; meals from SF 56
Rooms 26 double; all have bath or shower, phone, TV, radio, minibar, hairdrier, safe; some air-conditioned

Facilities 2 dining-rooms, sitting-room, bar, whirlpool, lift/elevator; terrace, garden, heated swimming-pool
Credit cards AE, DC, MC, V
Children welcome
Disabled not suitable
Pets accepted
Closed Jan, Feb
Languages English, French, German, Italian
Managers Piazzoli family

Ticino

Villa Magliasina

At first glance, our inspector thought this 60-year-old villa was a golf club, thanks to the 'private' sign on the gravel drive and the 18-hole course at the back. Certainly, the theme is golf, with old prints of Scotland on the walls and even a grass-green carpet in the entrance. Special 'golf weeks' allow enthusiasts to play some of the 15 courses in the area, transported by the hotel minibus. Not all guests, however, are golf fans. Some bicycle along the lakeside, others hike; Lugano is just a 20-minute ride on the local metro, while the lazy sunbathe by the heated swimming-pool.

Five bedrooms open straight on to the garden while those upstairs have balconies, such as 'Hybiscus' which overlooks a huge camelia. These 'flower rooms', recently-decorated in soft turquoise, grey and pink, make the others look rather boring by comparison. There is also simpler, and cheaper, accommodation in the annexe. Overall, the quiet, even staid atmosphere, suits couples more than families with small children who might not, for example, appreciate the series of Sunday classical music concerts. The prevalent scent of peach pot-pourri is deliberate: 'when guests smell that, we want them to remember us'.

Nearby lake, Lugano; golf, riding, tennis, walking, windsurfing.

6983 Magliaso-Lugano TI
Tel (091) 6112929
Fax (091) 6112920
Location in park; ample car parking, garages
Meals breakfast, lunch, dinner, snacks
Prices rooms S-SSS with breakfast
Rooms 17 double; 4 single; all have bath or shower, central heating, phone, TV, radio, minibar, hairdrier, safe
Facilities dining-room, sitting-room, bar; terrace, garden, heated swimming-pool, two practice holes, table-tennis
Credit cards AE, DC, MC, V
Children accepted
Disabled one adapted bedroom; ground floor access 5 rooms
Pets accepted
Closed Dec to just before Easter
Languages English, French, German, Italian
Manager Giorgio Zandona

Ticino

Lakeside hotel, Morcote

Carina Carlton

The lovely village of Morcote sits at the very tip of the Ceresio peninsula jutting into Lake Lugano. When the weather is fine, this is a very popular destination for a day out, with queues for tables at waterside restaurants. In such an attractive location, it would be all too easy for a hotelier to sit back and wait for customers to turn up. Not Rudolf Tschannen. Since he took over in 1990, improvements have been steady but gradual, from new colour schemes to new carpets.

Favourite rooms are numbers 35 and 36, where you can lie back in bed and look through tall windows, across the lake to the Italian border. Although the century-old house is right on the road, behind all is quiet in the steeply-terraced garden with palms, fig tree and a swimming-pool. High above stands the church of Santa Maria, whose cemetery is known for its monuments. Those who climb the 452 steps to look around should sleep soundly through the bells which ring 66 times at 6 am. There is a patio at the front for dining alfresco but most prefer to wait for a table across the road, to sit right over the water. Lit by candles at night, this is definitely a romantic spot.
Nearby lake; golf, tennis, riding, walking, casino in Italy.

6922 Morcote TI
Tel (091) 9961131
Fax (091) 9961929
Location overlooking lake in village; car parking difficult
Meals breakfast, lunch, dinner, snacks
Prices rooms SS-SSS with breakfast
Rooms 18 double; 3 suites; all have bath or shower, phone, TV, radio, minibar
Facilities 2 dining-rooms, 3 sitting-rooms, bar; terrace, garden, heated swimming-pool
Credit cards AE, DC, MC, V
Children welcome
Disabled not suitable
Pets accepted
Closed mid-Nov to mid-Feb
Languages English, French, German, Italian
Proprietors Tschannen family

Ticino

Village hotel, Ronco

Albergo Ronco

'Stunning views over Lake Maggiore' was our inspector's comment on this former hostel for the neighbouring convent. 'But you have to offer more than a great view,' insists Guido Casparis, the fourth generation of this family business. His father, Willi, provides the rival attraction. As chef, he makes all his own pasta, pastries, cakes, even the *grappa* from the vines which creep over the trellis above the granite terrace.

Ronco has always attracted artists and writers: Paulette Goddard was a regular at lunch-time, no doubt enjoying the cold *pesce carpione* (marinaded lake trout) followed by *frutta gratinata* (berries with vanilla sauce) that regulars order now. Our reporter liked the combination of simplicity and style. While locals sip a beer or coffee downstairs in the bar, with tiled floors and wooden chairs, upstairs all is quiet. Bedrooms are fresh-looking, with pink and blue furniture, white walls and oatmeal-coloured carpets. 'Some guests have been coming here for a month every summer for over 30 years,' according to Guido. 'Some explore the little villages, go walking or even drive to Milan. Others laze by the pool, taking in that view.'

Nearby Isole de Brissago, Madonna di Ponte; lake, walking.

6622 Ronco s/Ascona TI
Tel (091) 7915265
Fax (091) 7910640
Location in heart of village, next to church; ample car parking, some covered garages
Meals breakfast, lunch, dinner, snacks
Prices rooms S-SSS with breakfast
Rooms 14 double; 2 single; 4 suites; all have bath or shower, phone, TV, radio, safe
Facilities dining-room, sitting-room, bar; terrace, garden, swimming-pool
Credit cards AE, DC, MC, V
Children welcome
Disabled not suitable
Pets not accepted
Closed mid-Nov to mid-March
Languages English, French, German, Italian
Proprietors Casparis family

Ticino

Lakeside hotel, Ronco at Porto Ronco

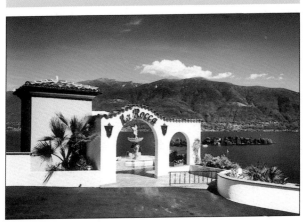

La Rocca

Visitors to the Island of Brissago have the best view of this hotel, tucked into the hillside below the road that winds steeply down to Porto Ronco, a writers' and artists' colony. 'Twenty years ago, this was just a pension with one bathroom and one telephone,' explains Felix Krähenmann, who wears the chef's hat. His wife, Dorothea, chose the furnishings. In the entrance, a small alcove by the bar is a cosy spot for coffee and cake, or to listen to the white piano while sipping a drink. Bedrooms overlook Lake Maggiore and are comfortable but not luxurious, with pale blue, green or yellow and cream providing a backdrop to the lacquered cane furniture. Some have balconies but all bear a 'welcome sign' with flowers to greet guests on their first night.

Whether you take a table inside or on the terrace under the wooden ceiling, the panorama is equally impressive. The only other houses in view are mere dots on the far side of the lake. Special evenings include 'Ticino' night, with accordion music and waitresses dressed in red and blue local costumes, and an outdoor barbecue in the garden, where banana, grapefruit, orange and palm trees provide an exotic touch.

Nearby lake; golf, tennis, riding, wind surfing.

6613 Porto Ronco, Ascona TI
Tel (091) 7915344
Fax (091) 7914064
E-mail Hotel@la-rocca.ch
Location hidden from view on twisting road between Ronco and the lake
Meals breakfast, lunch, dinner, snacks
Prices rooms SS-SSSS, with breakfast
Rooms 19 double; 2 suites; all have bath or shower, phone, TV, radio, minibar, safe

Facilities dining-room, sitting-room, bar, sauna and fitness area, lift/elevator; terrace, garden, indoor swimming-pool
Credit cards DC, MC, V
Children welcome
Disabled not suitable
Pets not accepted
Closed late Oct to mid-March
Languages English, French, German, Italian
Proprietors Krähenmann family

Ticino

Ristorante Motto del Gallo

'How can there be anything worthy of inclusion in the middle of an industrial zone wedged between the motorway and a main route through the valley?' our inspector asked herself as she followed signs to this well-known restaurant. She changed her mind upon seeing the 500-year-old farmhouse on a hill above the road and camouflaged by an apple orchard and a large cherry tree dripping with ripe fruit. Wooden roof tiles cover the wine press and stone fireplace in the former granary, while water trickles from a fountain into a horsetrough. With potted geraniums and strawberry plants, she half-expected a menu of rustic food.

Instead, she discovered one of the region's most inventive kitchens, where Nico and José Jglesias serve duck ravioli, brill with rhubarb, truffles and almond *crespelle* followed by hot soufflés for dessert. Upstairs, memories of old Ticino are revived with floral-patterned bedspreads brightening the three bedrooms, which have white walls, dark, old beams and decorative wrought-iron. 'Not the place for a week's holiday but a delightful overnight after a gourmet dinner' was her judgement.

Nearby Lake Lugano, Lugano; Bellinzona.

6807 Taverne-Lugano TI
Tel (091) 9452871
Fax (091) 9452723
Location south of the village of Taverne; ample car parking below hotel
Meals breakfast, lunch, dinner
Prices rooms SS-SSS with breakfast
Rooms 3 suites; all with bath/shower, fireplace
Facilities 2 dining-rooms, sitting-room, bar; terrace, garden
Credit cards AE, DC, MC, V
Children welcome
Disabled not suitable
Pets accepted
Closed 22 Dec to 20 Jan; restaurant only, Sun
Languages English, French, German, Italian, Spanish
Proprietors Nico and José De La Jglesia, Piero Tenca

Suisse Romande

❋ Chalet hotel, Château-d'Oex ❋

Bon Accueil

This 18thC chalet has everything that is 'typically Swiss': stone walls and old beams, deep leather armchairs and log fires, fine food and magnificent views over meadows and mountains. An excellent base for walking holidays and for families.

❖ 1837 Château-d'Oex VD **Tel** (026) 9246320 **Fax** (026) 9245126 **Meals** breakfast, lunch, dinner, snacks **Prices** rooms S-SSS with breakfast **Rooms** 21, all with bath or shower, central heating, phone, TV, radio **Credit cards** AE, DC, MC, V **Closed** Nov to mid-Dec; 4 weeks after Easter **Languages** English, French, German

---

Lakeside hotel, Cully

Major Davel

No cars block the view of the nearby peninsula, terraced with vines. The only noise is made by patrons of the bustling restaurant. Most bedrooms face the lake. Stay here if you cannot afford, or cannot get in to, the nearby Auberge du Raisin.

❖ 1096 Cully (Lavaux) VD **Tel** (021) 7999494 **Fax** (021) 7993782 **Meals** breakfast, lunch, dinner, snacks **Prices** rooms SS with breakfast **Rooms** 14, all with bath or shower, central heating, phone, TV, radio **Credit cards** AE, MC, V **Closed** never **Languages** English, French, German, Italian

---

Restaurant with rooms, Delémont

Du Midi

Hotels near stations are rarely attractive but Ghislain Pissenem runs an award-winning restaurant in the capital of the Jura. Choose between the brasserie, restaurant or gastronomic dining-room. Excellent fish, wines. Well-priced. Four pleasant bedrooms.

❖ 2800 Delémont JU **Tel** (032) 4221777 **Fax** (032) 4231989 **Meals** breakfast, lunch, dinner, snacks **Prices** rooms S-SS with breakfast **Rooms** 4, all with bath or shower, central heating, phone, TV, radio **Credit cards** AE, MC, V **Closed** mid-July to mid-Aug; Christmas; restaurant only, Wed **Languages** English, French, German, Italian

---

City hotel, Geneva

St Gervais

This is the sort of hotel budget travellers pray for: reasonably priced, very clean and only one minute from the main railway station and the lake. Entrance is through a small café, decoration is basic brown, but book well in advance.

❖ Corps-Saints 20, 1201 Geneva GE **Tel** (022) 7324572 **Meals** breakfast **Prices** rooms S-SS with breakfast **Rooms** 26, all with bath or shower, central heating, phone **Credit cards** AE, DC, MC, V **Closed** never **Languages** English, French, German, Italian

Suisse Romande

City hotel, Geneva

Tiffany

A friendly spot, with a popular restaurant, near the Grand Theatre and Stock Exchange. Despite its excessive art nouveau decoration, the Tiffany only opened in 1991. The modern bedrooms on the top floor have the most character.

❖ Rue de l'Arquebuse 18, 1204 Geneva GE **Tel** (022) 3293311 **Fax** (022) 3208991 **Meals** breakfast, lunch, dinner, snacks **Prices** rooms SSS-SSSS with breakfast **Rooms** 28, all with bath or shower, central heating, phone, TV, radio, minibar, hairdrier **Credit cards** AE, DC, MC, V **Closed** never **Languages** English, French, German, Italian

---

Lakeside hotel, Bellevue-Geneva

Port Gitana

What looks like little more than a large, elegant pizzeria hides some startling rooms with high ceilings under the eaves. Despite the busy restaurant, rooms are quiet with views over the small harbour and Geneva's famous fountain.

❖ 314 Route de Lausanne, 1293 Bellevue-Geneva GE **Tel** (022) 7743148 **Fax** (022) 7743352 **Meals** breakfast, lunch, dinner, snacks **Prices** rooms SS-SSS with breakfast **Rooms** 6, all with bath or shower, central heating, phone, TV, radio **Credit cards** AE, DC, MC, V **Closed** never **Languages** English, French, German, Italian

---

Town hotel, Geneva at Petit-Lancy

Hostellerie de la Vendée

The Righetto's business-oriented hotel in Lancy, on a hillside above Geneva, is best known for chef Stefan Taffonneau's cooking in the Pont-Rouge Restaurant with its new conservatory. Bedrooms, refurbished recently, provide city-style comforts.

❖ 1213 G-Petit-Lancy, Chemin de la Vendée 28 GE **Tel** (022) 7920411 **Fax** (022) 7920546 **Meals** breakfast, lunch, dinner **Prices** rooms SSS with breakfast **Rooms** 34, all with bath or shower, central heating, phone, TV, radio **Credit cards** AE, DC, MC, V **Closed** mid-Dec to early Jan; rest. only, Sat lunch, Sun **Languages** English, French, German

---

Old inn, Gruyères

La Fleur de Lys

The Yerly family took over in 1998 but changed little apart from lowering the prices in the 300-year old mansion, with beams and wood-panelling. Expect local cheese and dried meat, fondue, *raclette* and trout. Plain bedrooms.

❖ 1663 Gruyères FR **Tel** (029) 62108 **Fax** (029) 63605 **Meals** breakfast, lunch, dinner, snacks **Prices** rooms S-SS with breakfast **Rooms** 8, all with bath or shower, central heating, phone, TV, radio **Credit cards** AE, DC, MC, V **Closed** Feb; restaurant only, Tues (winter) **Languages** English, French, German

Suisse Romande

Lakeside hotel, Lausanne at St Sulpice

Hostellerie du Debarcadère

Once a modest pension, now a proud member of the Relais & Châteaux group with rich fabrics, smooth marble, fresh flowers. Despite the Kluvers' professionalism, many guests find the atmosphere too formal. Smiles would be welcome.

❖ 1025 St Sulpice VD **Tel** (021) 6915747 **Fax** (021) 6915079 **Meals** breakfast, lunch, dinner, snacks **Prices** rooms SS-SSSS with breakfast **Rooms** 15, all with bath or shower, central heating, phone, TV, radio **Credit cards** AE, DC, MC, V **Closed** never **Languages** English, French, German, Italian

Lake-view hotel, Veytaux near Montreux

Masson

The Sèvegrand-Jaquier family's hotel retains its 19thC features: polished parquet floors, a grand piano, brass bedsteads, walnut furniture. In wooded gardens with panoramic views over Lake Léman. The best rooms have balconies.

❖ 1820 Montreux-Veytaux VD **Tel** (021) 9660044 **Fax** (021) 9660036 **Meals** breakfast, dinner **Prices** rooms S-SSS with breakfast **Rooms** 30, all with bath or shower, central heating, phone, TV, radio **Credit cards** AE, MC, V **Closed** Nov to end March **Languages** English, French, German, Italian

Village inn, Vers-chez-Perrin

Auberge de Vers-chez-Perrin

In this hamlet near Payerne, Pierre-Dominique Linder's sophisticated country inn comes as a surprise until you learn that he was a student with Fredy Girardet. Superb meals, top-class wines. Bedrooms are comfortable and quiet in this rural retreat.

❖ 1551 Vers-chez-Perrin VD **Tel** (026) 6605846 **Meals** breakfast, lunch, dinner, snacks **Prices** rooms S-SS with breakfast **Rooms** 7, all with bath or shower, central heating, phone, TV, radio **Credit cards** not accepted **Closed** mid-July to mid-Aug; restaurant only, Mon, Sun evening **Languages** English, French, German

Bern

City hotel, Bern

Goldenen Adler

A budget hotel with an ancient exterior right in the heart of the city. Overall, rather dark inside. Contemporary, dull furniture in most bedrooms; those on the top floor, however, have paler colours and beamed ceilings. Locals use the small restaurant.

❖ 3011 Bern, Gerechtigkeitsgasse 7 BE **Tel** (031) 3111725 **Fax** (031) 3113761 **Meals** breakfast, lunch, dinner, snacks **Prices** rooms SS with breakfast **Rooms** 22, all with bath or shower, central heating **Credit cards** AE, DC, MC, V **Closed** never; restaurant only, Sun **Languages** English, French, German, Italian, Spanish

---

Airport hotel, Bern at Belp

Flughafen Belpmoos

Our aeroplane-mad inspector fell in love with this hotel, close to the control tower of a small airport. Thankfully, the planes stop at night. Modern, furnished in warm colours. Since the Maeders worked in France, food is excellent. Fair value.

❖ 3123 Bern-Belp BE **Tel** (031) 9616181 **Fax** (031) 9613168 **Meals** breakfast, lunch, dinner, snacks **Prices** rooms S-SS with breakfast **Rooms** 15, all with bath or shower, central heating, phone, TV, radio **Credit cards** AE, DC, MC, V **Closed** never **Languages** English, French, German, Italian, Spanish

---

Suburban hotel, Bern at Belp

Sternen

Another budget hotel near Bern. Our inspector compares it to an old-fashioned English pub: dark decoration and traditional food in big helpings. The Kübli-Schär family has two bowling alleys, so this is a place to meet the locals and the house parrot.

❖ 3123 Belp BE **Tel** (031) 8190011 **Fax** (031) 8190181 **Meals** breakfast, lunch, dinner, snacks **Prices** rooms S-SS with breakfast **Rooms** 18, all with bath or shower, central heating, phone, TV, radio **Credit cards** AE, DC, MC, V **Closed** never; restaurant only, Mon, Tues **Languages** English, French, German, Italian

---

Wayside inn, Boll near Bern

Zum Bären

Useful for the cost-conscious, since the local Bern-Worb commuter train stops nearby. The Gygax family prides itself on its links with the past and also run a *Metzgerei* (butcher's). The Bären is on the road, so ask for a room at the back.

❖ 3067 Boll bei Bern BE **Tel** (031) 8390470 **Fax** (031) 8396345 **Meals** breakfast, lunch, dinner, snacks **Prices** rooms S-SS with breakfast **Rooms** 6, all with bath or shower, central heating, phone, radio **Credit cards** AE, MC, V **Closed** never; restaurant only, Tues; Wed lunch **Languages** English, French, German

Bern

Wayside inn, Bern at Münsingen

Löwen

Recently renovated, this *Landgasthof* between Bern and Thun is quite grand with its spiral staircase. We like the bedroom under the eaves with its ship-like timbers. The quality of the cooking matches the elegance of the restaurant with its parquet floor.

❖ 3110 Münsingen, Bernstr 28 BE **Tel** (031) 724311 **Fax** (031) 7243110 **Meals** breakfast, lunch, dinner, snacks **Prices** rooms SF83-138 with breakfast **Rooms** 17, all with bath or shower, central heating, phone, TV, radio **Credit cards** AE, DC, MC, V **Closed** never **Languages** some English, French, German

---

Village hotel, Schönbühl near Bern

Schönbühl

The Gerber-Fuhrer family have had this inn since Schönbühl was a country village, nearly a century ago. The panelled walls are covered in photos of the local mayors. The mixture of antique and modern furniture combines well in this classic local hostelry.

❖ 3322 Schönbühl bei Bern BE **Tel** (031) 8596969 **Fax** (031) 8596905 **Meals** breakfast, lunch, dinner, snacks **Prices** rooms S-SS with breakfast **Rooms** 12, all with bath or shower, central heating, phone, TV, radio **Credit cards** AE, MC, V **Closed** Christmas; restaurant only, Wed English, French, German, Italian

---

Wayside inn, Langnau im Emmental

Hirschen

This 500-year-old tavern is now run by the Weyermann family and has benefited from redecoration. Comfortable rooms combined with reliable cooking. Well-priced.

❖ 3550 Langnau im Emmental BE **Tel** (034) 4021517 **Fax** (034) 402 25623 **Meals** breakfast, lunch, dinner, snacks **Prices** rooms S-SS with breakfast **Rooms** 17, all with bath or shower, central heating, phone, radio **Credit cards** AE, DC, MC, V **Closed** Jan; restaurant only, Mon; Tues lunch **Languages** English, French, German, Italian

---

City hotel, Thun

Emmental

Charles Lanzrein's 'café-hotel' is strictly contemporary after a recent facelift. The younger crowd comes for healthy snacks and salads in the convivial bar. Upstairs, bright new bedrooms have slick bathrooms with grey marble and pink tiles.

❖ 3600 Thun, Bernstr 2 BE **Tel** (033) 2220120 **Fax** (033) 2220130 **Meals** breakfast, lunch, dinner, snacks **Prices** rooms S-SS with breakfast **Rooms** 11, all with bath or shower, central heating, phone, TV, radio **Credit cards** AE, MC, V **Closed** never **Languages** English, French, German, Italian

Bern

Old inn, Thun

Krone

On the outside, the Krone could not look more Swiss with its spikey tower, tiled roof and shutters. Inside, bedroom furniture looks more suited to an office; downstairs, there are two surprises: a French-style bistro and a Chinese restaurant.

❖ 3600 Thun, Rathausplatz BE **Tel** (033) 228282 **Fax** (033) 2278890 **Meals** breakfast, lunch, dinner, snacks **Prices** rooms SS-SSS with breakfast **Rooms** 27, all with bath or shower, central heating, phone, radio; some TV **Credit cards** AE, DC, MC, V **Closed** never **Languages** English, French, German, Italian

---

Country inn, Ursenbach

Hirsernbad

When it comes to fair prices, few can match the Duss family's pretty, old inn. Bedrooms are rustic and inexpensive; the restaurant is the focus of attention. Children play happily in the garden while parents enjoy the food and excellent wines.

❖ 4937 Ursenbach BE **Tel** (062) 9653256 **Fax** (062) 9652093 **Meals** breakfast, lunch, dinner, snacks **Prices** rooms S-SS with breakfast **Rooms** 4, all with bath or shower, central heating, phone, TV, radio **Credit cards** MC, V **Closed** never **Languages** English, French, German

---

Old inn, Weissenburg

Alte Post

A surprisingly atmospheric 200-year-old inn in the Simmental valley, with bench seats by the fire, wood-panelled bedrooms, carved ceilings. By the river, this restored hostelry is popular with canoeists and skiers who appreciate the well-prepared food.

❖ 3764 Weissenburg Dorf BE **Tel** (033) 7831515 **Fax** (033) 7831578 **Meals** breakfast, lunch, dinner **Prices** rooms S-SS with breakfast **Rooms** 9, all with bath or shower, central heating **Credit cards** DC, MC, V **Closed** Nov; rest only Wed, Thur **Languages** English, French, German

---

❈ Resort hotel, Zweisimmen ❈

Sonnegg

Converted by the Imobersteg family in 1980, this solid, green-shuttered hotel is tranquil in summer, busy with cross-country skiers in winter. Close to Gstaad but reasonably priced, expect hearty local food but somewhat basic bathrooms.

❖ 3770 Zweisimmen BE **Tel** (033) 7222333 **Fax** (033) 7222354 **Meals** breakfast, lunch, dinner, snacks **Prices** rooms S-SS with breakfast **Rooms** 10, all with bath or shower, central heating, phone, TV, radio **Credit cards** AE, DC, MC, V **Closed** never **Languages** English, French, German, Italian

Northern Cantons

City hotel, Basel

Helvetia

Not the prettiest small hotel in town, but one with plenty of character, thanks to the popular Old Red Ox bar and the Chez Alain restaurant, best-known for its seafood. Bedrooms are city-slick. One minute from station and air terminal.

❖ 4051 Basel, Küchengasse 13 BS **Tel** (061) 2720688 **Fax** (061) 2720622 **Meals** breakfast, lunch, dinner, snacks **Prices** rooms SS-SSS with breakfast **Rooms** 17, all with bath or shower, central heating, phone, TV, radio **Credit cards** AE, DC, MC, V **Closed** never **Languages** English, French, German, Italian

---

Castle hotel, Böttstein

Schloss Böttstein

Near the chapel, this castle dates from 1250, but a rebuilding programme in 1974 produced 20 bedrooms with all of this century's requirements. The chef concentrates on what he calls 'an international menu with a French emphasis: fish, beef veal.'

❖ 5315 Böttstein AG **Tel** (056) 2691616 **Fax** (056) 2691666 **Meals** breakfast, lunch, dinner, snacks **Prices** rooms S-SS with breakfast **Rooms** 20, all with bath or shower, central heating, phone, TV, radio **Credit cards** AE, DC, MC, V **Closed** 21 Dec to 22 Jan; 2 weeks in Aug; restaurant only, Mon **Languages** English, French, German

---

Restaurant with rooms, Egerkingen

Kreuz

The Kreuz in Egerkingen is perfectly placed, a mere 45 minutes from Bern, Basel, Lucerne and Zurich. Chef Louis Bischofberger prepares traditional fare for the Bistro, modern dishes for the Cheminée Restaurant. Eat in the garden in summer.

❖ 4622 Egerkingen, Oltnerstr 71 SO **Tel** (062) 3980333 **Fax** (062) 3984340 **Meals** breakfast, lunch, dinner, snacks **Prices** rooms SF100-275 with breakfast **Rooms** 8, all with bath or shower, central heating, phone, TV, radio **Credit cards** AE, MC, V **Closed** never **Languages** English, French, German

---

Wayside inn, Kriegstetten

Sternen

Near the motorway exit for Kriegstetten, the Sternen is a fine example of the Romantik hotel group. The restaurants and Gaststube are elegantly panelled in 19thC style, with some Biedermeier antiques. Bedrooms are also tastefully furnished.

❖ 4566 Kriegstetten SO **Tel** (032) 6756111 **Fax** (032) 6756025 **Meals** breakfast, lunch, dinner, snacks **Prices** rooms SS-SSS with breakfast **Rooms** 23, all with bath or shower, central heating, phone, TV, radio **Credit cards** AE, DC, MC, V **Closed** never **Languages** English, French, German, Italian

 *Northern Cantons*

---

* Country hotel, Liestal *

Bad Schauenburg

This luxury hotel is deep in peaceful countryside, a few minutes from Liestal itself. Owner Fredi Häring maintains a top-class restaurant which attracts the affluent of Basel, who book for the terrace in summer, the elegant dining-room in winter.

❖ 4410 Liestal BL **Tel** (061) 9011202 **Fax** (061) 9011055 **Meals** breakfast, lunch, dinner, snacks **Prices** rooms SS-SSS with breakfast **Rooms** 34, all with bath or shower, central heating, phone, TV, radio **Credit cards** AE, DC, MC, V **Closed** never; restaurant only, Sun evening **Languages** English, French, German

---

Restaurant with rooms, Nürensdorf

Zum Bären

Popular with businessmen and women, thanks to Felix Eppisser's fine modern cooking at this restaurant, a handy 10-minute drive from Zurich-Kloten airport. The rooms offer a refreshing alternative to airport hotels.

❖ 8309 Nürensdorf, Alte Winterthurerstr 45 ZH **Tel** (01) 8383636 **Fax** (01) 8383646 **Meals** breakfast, lunch, dinner, snacks **Prices** rooms SS-SSS with breakfast **Rooms** 14, all with bath or shower, central heating, phone, TV, radio **Credit cards** AE, DC, MC, V **Closed** Christmas and New Year; restaurant only, Sun, Mon **Languages** English, French,

---

Village inn, Obererlinsbach

Hirschen

A few minutes from the middle of Aarau, this *Landgasthof* has become known for its food. A seminar building has been addded for business conferences. High standards set by owner Albert von Felten. Enterprising vegetarian dishes.

❖ 5016 Obererlinsbach SO **Tel** (062) 8573333 **Fax** (062) 8573300 **Meals** breakfast, lunch, dinner, snacks **Prices** rooms SS-SSS with breakfast **Rooms** 16, all with bath or shower, central heating, phone, TV, radio **Credit cards** AE, DC, MC, V **Closed** Christmas and New Year **Languages** English, French, German

---

Lakeside hotel, Obermeilen

Hirschen

If you live in Zurich and have a boat, then the Hirschen is the ideal spot; so head out, tie up and have lunch on the terrace. The attractive restaurant has a growing reputation, so it is worth having dinner and staying the night.

❖ 8706 Obermeilen, Seestr 856 ZH **Tel** (01) 9250500 **Fax** (01) 9250501 **Meals** breakfast, lunch, dinner, snacks **Prices** rooms S-SSS with breakfast **Rooms** 16, all with bath or shower, central heating, phone, TV, radio **Credit cards** AE, DC, MC, V **Closed** never; restaurant only, Mon **Languages** English, French, German, Italian

Northern Cantons

Country inn, Wallbach near Rheinfelden

Zum Schiff

Robert and Yvonne Wüthrich-Barth are the dynamic duo behind the renovated *Landgasthof* near the Rhine. Children love the horses, donkeys and rabbits. Indoors, food is the priority. Whimsical antiques downstairs but simple, very basic bedrooms.

❖ 4323 Wallbach AG **Tel** (061) 8611109 **Fax** (01) 8611307 **Meals** breakfast, lunch, dinner, snacks **Prices** rooms S-SS with breakfast **Rooms** 5, all with bath or shower, central heating, phone, TV, radio **Credit cards** AE, DC, MC, V **Closed** never **Languages** English, French, German

---

Town hotel, Solothurn

Roter Turm / Tour Rouge

This 40-year-old hotel is a useful base in the medieval city. Rooms are functional and modern to satisfy the businessmen who are the main clients. Ask for a bedroom that has been redecorated recently. The roof-top terrace has delightful views.

❖ 4500 Solothurn, am Marktplatz **SO Tel** (032) 6229621 **Fax** (032) 6229865 **Meals** breakfast, lunch, dinner, snacks **Prices** rooms SF90-210 with breakfast **Rooms** 35, all with bath or shower, central heating, phone, TV, radio **Credit cards** AE, DC, MC, V **Closed** never **Languages** English, French, German, Italian, Spanish

---

Lakeside hotel, Uetikon

Krone

Eat fish on the terrace overlooking the lake and the ferry stop or, in winter, sample Patrice Salamin's French-style cooking inside, in the restaurant. Bedrooms in this 200-year old hotel were modernised in 1987; views at the front but the back is quieter.

❖ 8707 Uetikon, Seestr 117 ZH **Tel** (01) 9204567 **Fax** (01) 9205130 **Meals** breakfast, lunch, dinner, snacks **Prices** rooms S-SS with breakfast **Rooms** 13, all with bath or shower, central heating, phone, TV, radio **Credit cards** AE, DC, MC, V **Closed** Christmas to late Jan; restaurant only Wed, Thurs **Languages** English, French, German, Italian

Central Cantons

Old hostelry, Altdorf

Goldener Schlüssel

The arrival of Otto-Benno Jauch in 1998 gave this 17thC inn a much-needed facelift. This is one to watch. In the pedestrianzed heart of town, the standard of comfort and dining has dramatically improved, as has the welcome. Excellent wine cellar.

❖ 6460 Altdorf, Schützengasse 9 UR **Tel** (041) 8712002 **Fax** (041) 8701167 **Meals** breakfast, lunch, dinner, snacks **Prices** rooms SS with breakfast **Rooms** 21, all with bath or shower, central heating, phone, TV, radio **Credit cards** MC, V **Closed** never **Languages** English, French, German, Italian

---

Lakeside hotel, Buochs

Krone

The Bamert-Odermatt family have a dedicated, if undemanding, clientele. Small children love the lawn and beach. We would like to see some fresh paint outside and more personality inside. Low prices for very simple but clean bedrooms, some without bath.

❖ 6374 Buochs NW **Tel** (041) 6200820 **Fax** (041) 6201729 **Meals** breakfast, lunch, dinner, snacks **Prices** rooms S-SS with breakfast **Rooms** 30, most with bath or shower, central heating, phone, TV, radio **Credit cards** AE, MC, V **Closed** never **Languages** English, French, German, Italian

---

Resort hotel, Gersau

Müller

This may look more like a Mediterranean hotel, with its white walls, yellow sunshades and blue railings, but Gersau is on the Vierwaldstättersee. With plenty of sport, the Rigi behind and a steamer stop outside, this is ideal for family holidays.

❖ 6442 Gersau, Seestr 26 SZ **Tel** (041) 8281919 **Fax** (041) 8281962 **Meals** breakfast, lunch, dinner, snacks **Prices** rooms SS-SSS with breakfast **Rooms** 30, all with bath or shower, central heating, phone, TV, radio **Credit cards** AE, DC, MC, V **Closed** never **Languages** English, French, German, Italian

---

Lakeside hotel, Gersau

Seehof / du Lac

A classic hotel, peaceful and rather old-fashioned. It stands right on the water, a small, wooded bay on the edge of Gersau. The Henzi-Wiget family are quite charming. Some guests fish; many never leave the south-facing terrace.

❖ 6442 Gersau SZ **Tel** (041) 8298300 **Fax** (041) 8298384 **Meals** breakfast, lunch, dinner, snacks **Prices** rooms S-SS with breakfast **Rooms** 24, all with bath or shower, central heating, phone, TV, radio **Credit cards** AE, DC, MC, V **Closed** late Oct, early May **Languages** English, French, German, Italian

Central Cantons

Town hotel, Lachen

Bären

With its geranium-filled boxes and road-side terrace, the Bären is a useful overnight stop just off the N3, on the south side of Lake Zurich. Old-fashioned, with simple comforts. Expect large portions and a chance to meet locals over a beer.

❖ 8853 Lachen am Zürichsee SZ **Tel** (055) 4519999 **Fax** (055) 4519995 **Meals** breakfast, lunch, dinner, snacks **Prices** rooms S-SS with breakfast **Rooms** 19, all with bath or shower, central heating, phone, TV, radio **Credit cards** AE, DC, MC, V **Closed** never **Languages** English, French, German, Italian

Harbourside hotel, Lachen

Al Porto

This surprisingly modern square block of a hotel sits right next to the small harbour on the Zürichsee. Downstairs, the Italian-style pizzeria and trattoria are always busy, upstairs, the plain, pink and white bedrooms have sweeping views over the water.

❖ 8853 Lachen am Zürichsee SZ **Tel** (055) 4517373 **Fax** (055) 4517374 **Meals** breakfast, lunch, dinner, snacks **Prices** rooms SS with breakfast **Rooms** 22, all with bath or shower, central heating, phone, TV, radio **Credit cards** AE, DC, MC, V **Closed** never **Languages** English, French, German, Italian

Bed-and-breakfast hotel, Lucerne

Ambassador

Handily-placed in the heart of the city, this brand-new hotel has modern furniture and decorations: bent-wood chairs and sliding windows. Run efficiently by the Zehnder-Heiniger family, so standards are high. Small terrace garden at rear.

❖ 6004 Lucerne, Zürichstr 3 LU **Tel** (041) 4108283 **Fax** (041) 4107178 **Meals** breakfast **Prices** rooms SS-SSSS with breakfast **Rooms** 31, all with bath or shower, central heating, phone, TV, radio **Credit cards** AE, DC, MC, V **Closed** never **Languages** English, French, German, Italian

City hotel, Lucerne

ᴡᴡᴡ. Baslertor .ch

In the old part of town, this four-star hotel offers the comforts city folk expect: big, squashy armchairs, a marble-topped cocktail bar and an intimate restaurant. The nice surprise is the garden terrace restaurant and heated outdoor swimming-pool.

❖ 6000 Lucerne, Pfistergasse 17 LU **Tel** (041) 2400918 **Fax** (041) 2402030 **Meals** breakfast, lunch, dinner, snacks **Prices** rooms S-SSS with breakfast **Rooms** 30, all with bath or shower, central heating, phone, TV, radio **Credit cards** AE, DC, MC, V **Closed** never **Languages** English, French, German, Italian

0412492222

Central Cantons

Restaurant with rooms, Lucerne at Meggen

Sonnegg

On the shores of Lake Lucerne, Chef Schmidli's restaurant is synonymous with fish. Although he specialises in fresh-water fish, he also has a deft touch with seafish. With only a handful of bedrooms, this makes a useful base for exploring the area.

❖ 6045 Meggen, Hauptstr 37 LU **Tel** (041) 3774400 **Fax** (041) 3774940 **Meals** breakfast, lunch, dinner, snacks **Prices** rooms S-SS with breakfast **Rooms** 9, all with bath or shower, central heating, phone, TV, radio **Credit cards** AE, DC, MC, V **Closed** never; restaurant only, Mon lunch, Sun **Languages** English, French, German

---

Village inn, Stans

Engel

If you want to stay in a village, near a baroque church, between lake and mountain, then Stans is ideal. The Engel is down-to-earth, with hearty portions in the *Stübli* and practical rather than pretty bedrooms upstairs. Useful when touring.

❖ 6370 Stans, am Dorfplatz NW **Tel** (041) 6191010 **Fax** (041) 6191011 **Meals** breakfast, lunch, dinner, snacks **Prices** rooms S-SS with breakfast **Rooms** 9, all with bath or shower, central heating, phone, TV, radio **Credit cards** AE, DC, MC, V **Closed** never; restaurant only, Sun, Mon **Languages** English, French, German, Italian

---

Village inn, Stans

Linde

Beat Müller has maintained the high culinary standards set by predecessor Herbert Huber. The dark wood-panelled restaurant attracts eager gourmets; the bedrooms are a bonus with Persian rugs on the floor and stylish, apricot-coloured curtains.

❖ 6370 Stans, am Dorfplatz NW **Tel** (041) 6190930 **Fax** (041) 6190948 **Meals** breakfast, lunch, dinner, snacks **Prices** rooms S-SS with breakfast **Rooms** 9, all with bath or shower, central heating, phone, TV, radio **Credit cards** AE, DC, MC, V **Closed** never; restaurant only, Sun, Mon **Languages** English, French, German

---

Lakeside hotel, Weggis

Gerbi

Built in 1987, this is an unashamedly modern resort hotel on Switzerland's 'Riviera'. The imaginative use of dark wood gives it some character, but this is essentially for families and active guests, with the lake and an indoor swimming-pool at the door.

❖ 6353 Weggis LU **Tel** (041) 3902727 **Fax** (041) 39300129 **Meals** breakfast, lunch, dinner, snacks **Prices** rooms SS-SSSS with breakfast **Rooms** 25, all with bath or shower, central heating, phone, TV, radio **Credit cards** AE, DC, MC, V **Closed** never **Languages** English, French, German, Italian

NE Cantons

Restaurant with rooms, Altnau

Im Schäfli

In a delightful lakeside village, the Wilhelms have an equally delightful small hotel, run by Rita, while Urs creates photogenic fish dishes for the restaurant. Quality is the watchword from fresh produce on the tables to the modern bedrooms upstairs.

❖ 8595 Altnau am Bodensee, Kaffeegasse 1 TG **Tel** (071) 6951847 **Fax** (071) 6953105 **Meals** breakfast, lunch, dinner, snacks **Prices** rooms SS-SSS with breakfast **Rooms** 4, all with bath or shower, central heating, phone, TV, radio **Credit cards** AE,V **Closed** mid-Jan to mid-Feb; restaurant only, Wed **Languages** English, French, German

---

Country inn, Amriswil

Hirschen

The small town of Amriswil is scarcely a tourist attraction but the quaint, old *Landgasthof* is a pleasant place to stay, thanks to the award-winning cooking of Erich Baumer. Since he learnt his trade in Ticino, there is an Italian influence.

❖ 8580 Amriswil, Weinfelderstr 80 TG **Tel** (071) 4117971 **Fax** (071) 4117975 **Meals** breakfast, lunch, dinner, snacks **Prices** rooms S-SS with breakfast **Rooms** 8, all with bath or shower, central heating, phone, TV, radio **Credit cards** AE, DC, MC, V **Closed** mid-July to mid-Aug; restaurant only, Mon, Sun evening **Languages** English, French, German, Italia

---

Wayside inn, Ermatigen

Adler

This towering, half-timbered inn is the oldest in Thurgau, dating from 1270. Rebuilt in 1500, famous guests include Napoleon III, after whom the restaurant is named. Dine on chef Albert's imaginative fish dishes, surrounded by antique wood-panelling.

❖ Dorfplatz, 8272 Ermatigen TG **Tel** (071) 6641133 **Meals** breakfast, lunch, dinner, snacks **Prices** rooms S-SS with breakfast **Rooms** 4, all with bath or shower, central heating, phone, radio **Credit cards** AE, DC, MC, V **Closed** mid-Jan to mid-Feb; restaurant only, Mon evening, Tues **Languages** English, French, German, Italian

---

Lakeside inn, Ermatigen

Hirschen

Yet another of Ermatigen's lovely old inns, the Hirschen looks onto sail-boats bobbing at anchor on Lake Constance. Diners flock to eat the Knus-April's fish and game dishes on a waterside terrace beneath white umbrellas and sycamore trees.

❖ 8272 Ermatigen TG **Tel** (071) 6641003 **Meals** breakfast, lunch, dinner, snacks **Prices** rooms SS with breakfast **Rooms** 4, all with bath or shower, central heating, phone, radio **Credit cards** AE, DC, MC, V **Closed** restaurant only, Mon, Tues **Languages** English, French, German, Italian

NE Cantons

Village hotel, Ermatigen

Seetal Fischstube

Kurt Ribi has his own fishery, so it is no suprise that his atmospheric old restaurant specialises in fish dishes. The ten-roomed hotel is a modern block next door. Located just 50 m from the lake in an old fishing village.

❖ 8272 Ermatigen TG **Tel** (071) 6641414 **Fax** (071) 6643214 **Meals** breakfast, lunch, dinner, snacks **Prices** rooms S-SS with breakfast **Rooms** 10, all with bath or shower, central heating, phone, TV, radio **Credit cards** MC, V **Closed** never; restaurant only, Mon (summer); Mon; Tues (winter) **Languages** English, French, German, Italian

Lakeside hotel, Kreuzlingen

Seegarten

Overlooking the yacht harbour, Peter Günter's highly-rated restaurant features local lake fish. The annexe, above the Nautic Bar, has five modern bedrooms, named for ocean liners. All are clinical pink and grey with dazzling white bathrooms.

❖ Promenadestr 40, 8280 Kreuzlingen TG **Tel** (071) 6642877 **Fax** (071) 6642944 **Meals** breakfast, lunch, dinner, snacks **Prices** rooms SF110-190 with breakfast **Rooms** 5, all with bath or shower, central heating, phone, TV, radio **Credit cards** MC, V **Closed** Christmas, late Jan to mid-Feb; restaurant only, Mon **Languages** English, French, German, Italian

Restaurant with rooms, Langrickenbach

Zum Löwen

In the old *Landgasthof* opposite the church, Robert Purri is a chef who is building a reputation for his French-style dishes. The two rooms are small, plain but well-priced. A useful spot for an overnight stay.

❖ 8585 Langrickenbach TG **Tel** (071) 6951867 **Fax** (072) 651871 **Meals** breakfast, lunch, dinner **Prices** rooms SS with breakfast **Rooms** 2, both with bath or shower, central heating, radio **Credit cards** AE, DC, MC, V **Closed** late Jan, late Jul to early Aug restaurant only, Sun dinner, Mon **Languages** English, French, German

Suburban hotel, Schaffhausen at Herblingen

Hirschen

Hotel Park Villa owner, Max Schlumpf opened the Hirschen, north-east of Schaffhausen, in 1993. There is a stylish restaurant and a piano in the elegant bar. Choose a bedroom under the beamed roof or one with a huge white-tiled bath. A find.

❖ 8207 Schaffhausen-Herblingen, Schlossstr 20 SH **Tel** (052) 6432323 **Fax** (052) 6432328 **Meals** breakfast, lunch, dinner, snacks **Prices** rooms S-SS with breakfast **Rooms** 9, all with bath or shower, central heating, phone, TV, radio **Credit cards** AE, DC, MC, V **Closed** never **Languages** English, French, German

NE Cantons

Lakeside hotel, Steckborn

Frohsinn

This brown and white half-timbered hotel has a vine-covered terrace overlooking the lake where visitors enjoy a wide range of fish dishes. The Labhart-Brasser family always seems to be busy. However, the 1960s decoration would benefit from an up-date.

❖ 8266 Steckborn TG **Tel** (052) 7611161 **Fax** (052) 7612821 **Meals** breakfast, lunch, dinner, snacks **Prices** rooms S-SS with breakfast **Rooms** 10, all with bath or shower, central heating, phone, radio **Credit cards** AE, DC, MC, V **Closed** never; restaurant only, Tues evening, Fri **Languages** English, French, German

---

Town hotel, Teufen

Zur Linde

Bright, white modernized hotel with a pretty garden shaded by a 400-year old lime, or linden, tree. Popular with business travellers, useful as a base for the Appenzell region. Excellent disabled access. The restaurant enjoys a growing reputation.

❖ 9053 Teufen AR **Tel** (071) 3332822 **Fax** (071) 3334120 **Meals** breakfast, lunch, dinner, snacks **Prices** rooms S-SS with breakfast **Rooms** 14, all with bath or shower, central heating, phone, TV, radio **Credit cards** AE, DC, MC, V **Closed** never **Languages** English, French, German, Italian

---

❋ Village inn, Wald-Schönengrund ❋

Chäseren

This ochre guest-house is decorated inside and out in Appenzell style. At the edge of the village, the Bruderer family hosts hikers and skiers in bedrooms that are rustic but boast all modern conveniences. Book, tape and video cassette library downstairs.

❖ 9105 Wald-Schönengrund AR **Tel** (071) 3611751 **Fax** (071) 3611759 **Meals** breakfast, lunch, dinner, snacks **Prices** rooms SS-SSS with breakfast **Rooms** 18, all with bath or shower, central heating, phone, TV, radio **Credit cards** AE, DC, MC, V **Closed** never **Languages** English, French, German

Liechtenstein

❋ Chalet hotel, Malbun ❋

Malbunerhof

Only 25 years old and popular with families. The open-plan ground floor has a big fireplace, plenty of built-in seating, and a U-shaped bar. Minutes from the slopes, coffee and cakes are served after skiing. An impressive indoor swimming-pool.

❖ 9497 Malbun FL **Tel** (0423) 2632944 **Fax** (0423) 2639561 **Meals** breakfast, lunch, dinner, snacks **Prices** rooms S-SSS with breakfast **Rooms** 29, all with bath or shower, central heating, phone, TV, radio **Credit cards** AE, DC, MC, V **Closed** mid-Oct to Mid-Dec; after Easter to early June **Languages** English, French, German, Italian

---

Suburban hotel, Schaan

Sylva im Sax

On a hillside above the main road, the boring exterior belies rather plush furnishings. Ask for one of the bedrooms overlooking the quiet, tree-shaded garden. The atmosphere of the bar and dining-room is more 'business' than 'holiday'.

❖ Saxgasse 6, 9494 Schaan FL **Tel** (0423) 2323942 **Fax** (0423) 2328247 **Meals** breakfast, lunch, dinner, snacks **Prices** rooms SS with breakfast **Rooms** 8, all with bath or shower, central heating, phone, TV, radio, minibar **Credit cards** AE, DC, MC, V **Closed** never **Languages** English, French, German, Italian

---

Restaurant with rooms, Triesen

Schatzmann

Klaus Schatzmann has built up a reputation for fine cooking and delights in adapting traditional recipes to suit modern tastes. The 12 original bedrooms are plain and simple; greater comfort in the new annexe, which opened in 1994.

❖ 9495 Triesen FL **Tel** (0423) 3991212 **Fax** (0423) 3991210 **Meals** breakfast, lunch, dinner, snacks **Prices** rooms SS-SSS with breakfast **Rooms** 29, all with bath or shower, central heating, phone, TV, radio **Credit cards** AE, DC, MC, V **Closed** Christmas, New Year **Languages** English, French, German, Italian

---

❋ Resort hotel, Triesenberg ❋

Nürnberger's Martha Bühler

This hotel is named for the first woman to compete for Liechtenstein in the Winter Olympics. Downstairs, panelling predominates; upstairs, new bedrooms are an improvement on the old. Fair value for basic comforts.

❖ Sennwies 15, 9497 Triesenberg FL **Tel** (0423) 2374777 **Fax** (0423) 2374770 **Meals** breakfast, lunch, dinner, snacks **Prices** rooms S-SS, breakfast extra **Rooms** 14, all with bath or shower, central heating, phone, TV, radio **Credit cards** AE, DC, MC, V **Closed** after New Year to mid-Feb **Languages** English, French, German, Italian

Graubünden

※ Resort hotel, Arosa ※

Anita

This unprepossessing cream and brown concrete block hides one of the great wine cellars of the world. Beat Caduff is also an excellent cook, but it is his knowledge of wine that is legendary. The pleasant hotel is comfortable but plain.

❖ 7050 Hohe Promenade, Arosa, GR **Tel** (081) 3771109 **Fax** (081) 3773618 **Meals** breakfast, lunch, dinner, snacks **Prices** rooms SS-SSSS with breakfast **Rooms** 32, all with bath or shower, central heating, phone, TV, radio **Credit cards** not accepted **Closed** mid-Oct to mid-Dec; after Easter to mid-June **Languages** English, French, German, Italian

---

※ Resort hotel, Celerina ※

Hotel Saluver

Although only 12 years old, photographs of bob-sledders and racing drivers confirm that this is already a popular hotel for sport lovers. Christian Jurczyk's tempting cooking and cheerful staff make this a jolly holiday destination.

❖ 7505 Celerina GR **Tel** (081) 8331314 **Fax** (081) 8330681 **Meals** breakfast, lunch, dinner, snacks **Prices** rooms SS-SSS with breakfast **Rooms** 16, all have bath or shower, central heating, phone, radio **Credit cards** AE, DC, MC, V **Closed** never **Languages** English, French, German, Italian

---

※ Wayside inn, Churwalden ※

Hotel Post

Mr and Mrs Zegg-Held run this 385-year-old inn enthusiastically and have built a reputation for cheerful hospitality and imaginative food served in the sophisticated wood-panelled restaurant. Ideal base for family holidays in winter or summer.

❖ 7075 Churwalden GR **Tel** (081) 3821109 **Fax** (081) 3822213 **Meals** breakfast, lunch, dinner, snacks **Prices** rooms S-SS with breakfast **Rooms** 17, all with bath or shower, central heating, phone, TV, radio, minibar **Credit cards** AE, DC, MC, V **Closed** 2 weeks Nov; May **Languages** English, French, German, Italian

---

※ Town hotel, Davos Platz ※

Alte Post

Parts of this former post hotel date back to the 17thC but recent redecoration makes it prettier than ever. The cosy Tafaaser Schtuba restaurant is panelled in honey-coloured pine; bedrooms are small with a pink and grey theme.

❖ 7270 Davos Platz, Berglistutz 4 GR **Tel** (081) 4135403 **Fax** (081) 4135403 **Meals** breakfast, lunch, dinner, snacks **Prices** rooms S-SSS with breakfast **Rooms** 17, all with bath or shower, central heating, phone, TV, radio **Credit cards** AE, MC, V **Closed** never **Languages** English, French, German, Italian

Graubünden

❋ Town hotel, Davos ❋

Bündnerhof

This would be just another straightforward, square hotel but for the cheerful Fleury family. Expect hearty meals and basic comforts, with no frills. In quiet part of Davos, next to the ice stadium. Congress and sports centre a few steps away.

❖ 7270 Davos Platz GR **Tel** (081) 4135630 **Fax** (081) 4131177 **Meals** breakfast, lunch, dinner, snacks **Prices** rooms S-SSSS with breakfast **Rooms** 25, all with bath or shower, central heating, phone, TV, radio, minibar, safe **Credit cards** AE, MC, V **Closed** mid-Oct to mid-Dec; after Easter to mid-June **Languages** English, French, German, Italian

❋ Chalet hotel, Davos ❋

Hotel Larix

Above Davos, away from the bustle, the only chalet-style hotel left in this resort retains its old-fashioned feel of a private house, thanks to the Henderson family's furniture and pictures. Ski down to the Jakobshorn-Bahnen. Tennis nearby.

❖ 7270 Davos-Platz, Albertistr 9 GR **Tel** (081) 4131188 **Fax** (081) 4133349 **Meals** breakfast, lunch, dinner, snacks **Prices** SS-SSSS **Rooms** 20, all have bath or shower, central heating, phone, TV, radio **Credit cards** AE, DC, MC, V **Closed** after Easter to mid-June; early Oct to mid-Nov **Languages** English, French, German, Italian

❋ Restaurant with rooms, Davos at Laret ❋

Hubli's Landhaus

Felix Hubli's delicious dishes attract food-lovers from Davos, 5 km away. Of the plain but comfortable bedrooms in the annexe across the road (joined by a tunnel) numbers 30-35 are quietest, overlooking meadows. Special gourmet, off-piste ski weeks.

❖ 7265 Davos-Laret GR **Tel** (081) 4162121 **Fax** (081) 4163342 **Meals** breakfast, lunch, dinner **Prices** rooms S-SSSS with breakfast **Rooms** 20, all have bath or shower, central heating, phone, TV, radio **Credit cards** AE, DC, MC, V **Closed** after Easter to late May; Nov to mid-Dec; restaurant only, Mon **Languages** English, French, German, Italian

❋ Modern hotel, Flims ❋

Curtgin

The Moser family's hotel was built in 1980 but has all the carved wood and beams that visitors expect in chalet-style lodgings. Advantages include seclusion, away from the busy main street, and proximity to the main ski-lifts, two minutes walk away.

❖ 7017 Flims-Dorf GR **Tel** (081) 9113566 **Fax** (081) 9113455 **Meals** breakfast, lunch, dinner, snacks **Prices** rooms S-SSS with breakfast **Rooms** 25, all with bath or shower, central heating, phone, TV, radio **Credit cards** not accepted **Closed** Nov to mid-Dec; after Easter to mid-June **Languages** English, French, German, Italian

Graubünden

❊ Modern hotel, Flims ❊

Surpunt

An old villa that has been expanded, the Caduff family's hotel is popular with locals who drop in for dinner in the pretty restaurant. In summer, yellow sunshades dot the large garden; in winter, the main ski-lifts are ten minutes away.

❖ 7018 Flims-Waldhaus GR **Tel** (081) 9111169 **Fax** (081) 9113817 **Meals** breakfast, lunch, dinner, snacks **Prices** rooms S-SSS with breakfast **Rooms** 27, all with bath or shower, central heating, phone, TV, radio **Credit cards** MC, V **Closed** Nov to mid-Dec; after Easter to mid-May **Languages** English, French, German, Italian

---

❊ Mountain hotel, Flims at Fidaz ❊

Fidazerhof

Roland Häfliger and Antonia Schärli took over this popular old hotel above Flims in 1993. Offering reflexology and massage, vegetarian dishes (but no pork), the young couple are building a new health and fitness image. One to watch.

❖ 7017 Flims-Fidaz GR **Tel** (081) 9113503 **Fax** (081) 9112175 **Meals** breakfast, lunch, dinner, snacks **Prices** rooms S-SSSS with breakfast **Rooms** 14, all with bath or shower, central heating, phone, radio **Credit cards** AE, DC, MC, V **Closed** never **Languages** English, French, German, Italian

---

❊ Pension, Ftan ❊

La Tschuetta

Silvia and Heribert Dietrich are the new owners of what looks and feels like a private house in the charming old mountain hamlet of Ftan Pitschen. Ask for full directions. There are no signs. Delightful restaurant.

❖ 7551 Ftan GR **Tel** (081) 8641230 **Fax** (081) 8648068 **Meals** breakfast, lunch, dinner, snacks **Prices** rooms SS-SSS with breakfast **Rooms** 4, all with bath or shower, central heating, phone, TV, radio **Credit cards** MC, V **Closed** mid-Oct to mid-Dec; after Easter to mid-Jun; restaurant only Mon, Tues **Languages** English, French, German, Italian

---

❊ Village inn, Guarda ❊

Piz Buin

A jolly, busy, rustic hotel at the end of the village where Herr Rubi's local dishes such as *Plain in Pigna* (a potato, egg and bacon dish) and *Tuorton* (meat loaf) draw hikers to the restaurant with its big picture windows. Plain, comfortable bedrooms.

❖ 7545 Guarda GR **Tel** (081) 8622424 **Fax** (081) 8622404 **Meals** breakfast, lunch, dinner, snacks **Prices** rooms S-SS with breakfast **Rooms** 22, all with bath or shower, central heating **Credit cards** DC, MC, V **Closed** Nov to mid-Dec; May to mid-June **Languages** English, French, German, Italian

Graubünden

❈ Converted farm, Klosters Dorf ❈

Rätia

Since 1976, the Burckhards have transformed a farm into today's popular and informal hotel. Cowsheds were converted into bedrooms and a restaurant, with massive beams and fireplace. Many rooms overlook broad meadows on the edge of Klosters.

❖ 7252 Klosters Dorf **Tel** (081) 4224747 **Fax** (081) 4224749 **Meals** breakfast, lunch, dinner, snacks **Prices** rooms S-SSS with breakfast **Rooms** 22, all with bath or shower, central heating, phone, radio, minibar **Credit cards** AE, DC, MC, V **Closed** mid-Oct to mid-Dec; after Easter to mid-June **Languages** English, French, German, Italian

---

❈ Village hotel, Lenzerheide ❈

Hotel Spescha

This brand-new hotel faces the road but the bedrooms, complete with traditional pale wood and fresh-looking floral curtains, are at the rear looking on to the hillside. Both guests and locals enjoy coffee and cakes in the café and meals in the Bündnerstübli.

❖ 7078 Lenzerheide GR **Tel** (081) 3846263 **Fax** (081) 3845140 **Meals** breakfast, lunch, dinner, snacks **Prices** rooms S-SSSS with breakfast **Rooms** 12, all have bath or shower, central heating, phone, TV, radio **Credit cards** MC **Closed** May **Languages** English, French, German, Italian

---

❈ Resort hotel, Pontresina ❈

Kochendörfer's Albris

The great attraction is the cake and pastry shop at the entrance where three generations of Kochendörfers have also made their own chocolates. Recently renovated, the bedrooms have plenty of light wood, brightly patterned curtains and carpets.

❖ 7504 Pontresina Gr **Tel** (081) 8388040 **Fax** (081) 8388050 **Meals** breakfast, lunch, dinner, snacks **Prices** rooms SF110-230 with breakfast **Rooms** 35, all with bath or shower, central heating, phone, radio, safe **Credit cards** DC, MC, V **Closed** mid-Oct to mid-Dec; after Easter to mid-June **Languages** English, French, German, Italian

---

❈ Wayside inn, Savognin ❈

Piz Mitgel

Eccentric, yet appealing, this old hotel was carefully renovated by the Waldegg family. Where else can you breakfast in a former ballroom or collect mountain herbs and flowers with a herbalist? Bedrooms include split-level 'maisonettes' that can sleep four.

❖ 7460 Savognin GR **Tel** (081) 6841161 **Fax** (081) 6843278 **Meals** breakfast, lunch, dinner, snacks **Prices** rooms S-SS with breakfast **Rooms** 30, all with bath or shower, central heating, phone, TV, radio **Credit cards** AE, DC, MC, V **Closed** Nov to mid-Dec; 4 weeks after Easter **Languages** English, French, German, Italian

Graubünden

❊ Bed-and-breakfast hotel, St Moritz ❊

Landguard

One glance at the trophies and you know the Trivellas are champion skiers. Their practical hotel has just been given a face-lift, so bedrooms such as numbers 10, 18 and 25 have been enlarged and have views over the lake. On a quiet back street.

❖ 7500 St Moritz GR **Tel** (081) 8333137 **Fax** (081) 8334546
Meals breakfast **Prices** rooms S-SSSS with breakfast
Rooms 21, all with bath or shower, central heating, phone, TV, radio, safe **Credit cards** AE, DC, MC, V **Closed** Nov to early Dec; May to mid-June **Languages** English, French, German, Italian, Spanish

---

❊ Villa hotel, Vulpera ❊

Villa Maria

Eat breakfast while watching putts being made on the second green of the nine-hole golf course that surrounds this hillside hotel. It is a former summer villa with too many pictures and ornaments but food is imaginative and the gardens are a delight.

❖ 7552 Vulpera GR **Tel** (081) 8641138 **Fax** (081) 8649161
Meals breakfast, lunch, dinner, snacks **Prices** rooms SS-SSSS with breakfast **Rooms** 15, all with bath or shower, central heating, phone, TV, radio, minibar, safe **Credit cards** MC, V **Closed** Nov to mid-Dec; after Easter to late May **Languages** English, French, German, Italian

---

❊ Village inn, Zuoz ❊

Crusch Alva

Chef Peter Jörimann has a considerable reputation in the EngadineValley, producing modern versions of local dishes. The pale green gourmet restaurant with deep-blue *Kachelofen* is very pretty. Old-word atmosphere.

❖ 7524 Zuoz GR **Tel** (081) 8541319 **Fax** (081) 8542459
Meals breakfast, lunch, dinner, snacks **Prices** rooms S-SS with breakfast **Rooms** 13, all with bath or shower, central heating, phone, radio **Credit cards** AE, DC, MC, V **Closed** mid-May to mid-June; 3 weeks Dec **Languages** English, French, German, Italian

Valais

❊ Lakeside hotel, Champex-Lac ❊

Glacier

This 100-year-old, lakeside hotel is ideal for families. Plenty of activities on offer, from tennis to fishing, and in winter, cross-country skiing. Mountaineers have always been regulars, welcomed by four generations of the Biselx family.

❖ 1938 Champex-Lac VS **Tel** (027) 7831402 **Fax** (027) 7833202 **Meals** breakfast, lunch, dinner, snacks **Prices** rooms S-SS with breakfast **Rooms** 28, all with bath or shower, central heating, phone, TV, radio **Credit cards** AE, DC, MC, V **Closed** Nov to mid-Dec; after Easter to end May **Languages** English, French, German, Italian

---

Riverside hotel, Chippis

Les Berges

Don't be put off by the fact that this hotel's restaurant was once a slaughter house. Popular with business travellers as well as holiday-makers. On the banks of the River Rhône and useful for an overnight stay. Well priced.

❖ 3965 Chippis VS **Tel** (027) 4522100 **Fax** (027) 4522129 **Meals** breakfast, lunch, dinner, snacks **Prices** rooms S-SS with breakfast **Rooms** 18, all with bath or shower, central heating, phone, TV, radio **Credit cards** AE, DC, MC, V **Closed** never; restaurant only, Sun evening **Languages** English, French, German, Italian

---

❊ Village hotel, Grimentz ❊

Moiry

Grimentz is one of the prettiest villages in the Valais, 1600 m up the unspoiled Val d'Anniviers. Hotels here cater for hikers and skiers, but the Salamin-Walker family provides large meals and comfortable, plain bedrooms. Book into the chalet-style annexe.

❖ 3961 Grimentz VS **Tel** (027) 4751144 **Fax** (027) 4752823 **Meals** breakfast, lunch, dinner, snacks **Prices** rooms SF50-105 with breakfast **Rooms** 16, all with bath or shower, central heating, radio **Credit cards** AE, DC, MC, V **Closed** after Easter; late Nov **Languages** English, French, German, Italian

---

❊ Modern hotel, Martigny ❊

Le Forum

Olivier and André Vallotton's cooking is among the finest in the Valais, so one scarcely notices the typically 1960s-style architecture. Add in the warm welcome and it is no surprise to find this is a popular stopover on the road from Italy to France.

❖ 1920 Martigny, Av du Grand-St-Bernard VS **Tel** (027) 7221841 **Fax** (027) 7227925 **Meals** breakfast, lunch, dinner **Prices** rooms S-SS with breakfast **Rooms** 29, all with bath or shower, central heating, phone, TV, radio **Credit cards** AE, DC, MC, V **Closed** 1 week Jan; rest. only, Sun eve, Mon **Languages** English, French, German, Italian

Valais

❉ Resort hotel, Saas Fee ❉

Allalin

Tobias Zurbriggen transformed this 70-year-old hotel, adding broad balconies and modern furniture to bedrooms. The 11 split-level suites are popular with families. Local paintings, carvings and wood panelling give the public rooms character.

❖ 3906 Saas Fee VS **Tel** (027) 9571815 **Fax** (027) 9573115 **Meals** breakfast, lunch, dinner, snacks **Prices** rooms S-SSSS with breakfast **Rooms** 27, all with bath or shower, central heating, phone, TV, radio **Credit cards** AE, DC, MC, V **Closed** never **Languages** English, French, German, Italian, Spanish

❉ Forest hotel, Saas Fee ❉

Fletschhorn

Irma Dütsch prepares exquisite French dishes for the rustic, pink and brown restaurant high above Saas Fee and deep in the silent pine forest. Bedrooms are delightfully old-fashioned with flowery fabrics and antique furniture. At 1800 m, views are breathtaking.

❖ 3906 Saas Fee VS **Tel** (027) 9572131 **Fax** (027) 9572187 **Meals** breakfast, lunch, dinner, snacks **Prices** rooms SSS-SSSS with breakfast **Rooms** 15, all with bath or shower, central heating, phone, TV, radio **Credit cards** AE, DC, MC, V **Closed** mid-Oct to mid-Dec; end April to mid-June **Languages** English, French, German

❉ Restaurant with rooms, Saas Fee ❉

Zur Mühle

Ariette Welti's grandfather was one of Saas Fee's first mountain guides. Now the Mühle is one of the most popular restaurants in town, with its red banquettes and pink table-cloths. The three bedrooms look out over the ski-slopes and glacier.

❖ 3906 Saas Fee VS **Tel** (027) 9572676 **Meals** breakfast, lunch, dinner, snacks **Prices** rooms S-SS with breakfast **Rooms** 3, all with bath or shower, central heating, phone, TV, radio **Credit cards** AE, DC, MC, V **Closed** mid-Oct to mid-Dec; May, June **Languages** English, French, German, Italian

❉ Chalet hotel, Vercorin ❉

Victoria

The Delft china and antiques in the dining-room reflect the Dutch origins of the Wagemakers but the owners' 17thC cellar restaurant is in true Valais-style, with *raclette* and wine. Bedrooms have hand-painted beds and cupboards.

❖ 3967 Vercorin VS **Tel** (027) 4554055 **Fax** (027) 4554057 **Meals** breakfast, lunch, dinner, snacks **Prices** rooms S-SS with breakfast **Rooms** 14, all with bath or shower, central heating, phone, TV, radio **Credit cards** AE, DC, MC, V **Closed** mid-Oct to mid-Nov; mid-April to mid-June **Languages** English, French, German, Dutch

Valais

❊ Village hotel, Vissoie ❊

Manoir de la Poste

The Melly-Bourgeois family go out of their way to spoil guests at this traditional inn. The proprietor has a bad back, so all bedrooms have articulated beds. Murals of local scenes, such as the 'fighting cows' of the Valais, feature in the dining-room.

❖ 3961 Vissoie VS **Tel** (027) 4751220 **Meals** breakfast, lunch, dinner, snacks **Prices** rooms S-SS with breakfast **Rooms** 10, all with bath or shower, central heating, phone, TV, radio **Credit cards** MC, V **Closed** mid-Nov to mid-Dec; June **Languages** English, French, German, Italian, Spanish

❊ Wayside inn, Vouvry ❊

Auberge de Vouvry

The rooms may be simple in this small 18thC inn near the French border, but Martial Brändle's modern versions of traditional Valais dishes enjoy a growing reputation. The village of Vouvry is on the main road, so demand a bedroom at the back.

❖ 1896 Vouvry, Place de l'Auberge VS **Tel** (024) 4811221 **Fax** (024) 4811754 **Meals** breakfast, lunch, dinner, snacks **Prices** rooms S-SS with breakfast **Rooms** 12, all with bath or shower, central heating, phone **Credit cards** MC, V **Closed** never; restaurant only, Sun evening, Mon **Languages** English, French, German, Italian

❊ Mountain hotel, Zermatt ❊

Riffelalp

The nearby Anglican chapel is a reminder of the British visitors who arrived at the original hotel by mule a century ago. The 1988 building is being completely renovated and enlarged.

❖ Riffelalp, 3920 Zermatt VS **Tel** (027) 9664646 **Fax** (027) 9675109 **Meals** breakfast, lunch, dinner, snacks **Prices** DB&B SS-SSS **Rooms** 20, all with bath or shower, central heating, phone **Credit cards** AE, DC, MC, V **Closed** Oct to mid-Dec; after Easter to end June **Languages** English, French, German, Italian

❊ Village hotel, Zinal ❊

Le Besso

At the top of the Val d'Anniviers, this 100-year-old stone inn has been carefully renovated by Jimmy and Marlene Casada. He is a keen walker and enjoys taking guests on hikes. Eat dinner while admiring the view of the Matterhorn and glacier.

❖ 3961 Zinal VS **Tel** (027) 4753165 **Fax** (027) 4754982 **Meals** breakfast, lunch, dinner, snacks **Prices** rooms S-SS with breakfast **Rooms** 10, all with bath or shower, central heating, phone **Credit cards** AE, DC, MC, V **Closed** Nov; May **Languages** English, French, German, Italian

Ticino

Town hotel, Ascona

Hotel Riposo

In the pedestrianised old quarter but away from the bustle of the lake front, this boasts a garden and small swimming-pool on the roof-top terrace with views of the lake. Plain bedrooms and corridors are brightened with works by local painters and potters.

❖ 6612 Ascona, Scalinata della Ruga 4 TI **Tel** (091) 7913164 **Fax** (091) 7914663 **Meals** breakfast, lunch, dinner, snacks **Prices** rooms SS-SSS with breakfast **Rooms** 32, all have bath or shower, phone, radio **Credit cards** AE, DC, MC, V **Closed** mid-Oct to just before Easter; after Easter to mid-June **Languages** English, French, German, Italian

Lakeside hotel, Gandria

Hotel Moosmann

Down 59 steep steps, this simple place is on the water with glorious views south to Italy. Wedged between Lake Lugano and the old village where visitors have to park and walk down the narrow lane. Plain bedrooms; grills and pasta in the restaurant.

❖ 6978 Gandria TI **Tel** (091) 9717261 **Fax** (091) 9727132 **Meals** breakfast, lunch, dinner, snacks **Prices** rooms S-SSS with breakfast **Rooms** 30, all have bath or shower, phone, radio, minibar **Credit cards** AE, DC, MC, V **Closed** mid-Nov to mid-March **Languages** English, French, German, Italian

Bed-and-breakfast hotel, Locarno

Piccolo Hotel

Recent redecoration makes this turn-of-the-century villa a find. Unusually elegant, the Piccolo is powder-blue and white outside and carpeted inside in smart coffee-cream. Floral and butterfly prints cover the walls; bathrooms sparkling white and modern.

❖ 6600 Locarno-Muralto, Via A. Buetti 11 TI **Tel** (091) 7430212 **Fax** (091) 7432198 **Meals** breakfast **Prices** rooms S-SS with breakfast **Rooms** 20, all have bath or shower, phone, TV, radio **Credit cards** AE, DC, MC, V **Closed** Nov to Easter **Languages** English, French, German, Italian

Resort hotel, Locarno

Zurigo

Green shutters and wrought-iron balconies give distinction to this white block at the Muralto end of the lake front. Busy café under spreading chestnut trees. Don't be put off by the dark green corridors; bedrooms are bright and white. Handy base.

❖ 6600 Locarno, Viale Verbano 9 TI **Tel** (091) 7431617 **Fax** (091) 7434315 **Meals** breakfast, lunch, dinner, snacks **Prices** rooms S-SSS with breakfast **Rooms** 28, all have shower, phone, TV, radio **Credit cards** AE, DC, MC, V **Closed** Jan **Languages** English, French, German, Italian

Ticino

Resort hotel, Lugano at Aldesago

Colibrì

Sunbathers lounging by the kidney-shaped swimming-pool enjoy the same panoramic view south over Lake Lugano as do diners in the long restaurant and guests in lakeside bedrooms. Brass and glass inside, the look is 'modern seaside'.

❖ Via Bassone 7, 6974 Aldesago-Lugano TI **Tel** (091) 9714242 **Fax** (091) 9719016 **Meals** breakfast, lunch, dinner, snacks **Prices** rooms S-SSS with breakfast **Rooms** 30, all with bath or shower, phone, TV, radio **Credit cards** MC, V **Closed** Jan, Feb **Languages** English, French, German, Italian

---

Suburban villa, Comano near Lugano

La Comanella

Mrs. Hartmann's paintings of clowns greet visitors to this square, modern hotel in the chestnut forests above Lugano, where businessmen and holiday-makers enjoy the seclusion of a small village. More home than hotel.

❖ 6949 Comano, near Lugano TI **Tel** (091) 9416571 **Fax** (091) 9426513 **Meals** breakfast, lunch, dinner, snacks **Prices** rooms S-SSS with breakfast **Rooms** 22, all have bath or shower, central heating, phone, TV, radio **Credit cards** AE, DC, MC, V **Closed** never **Languages** English, French, German, Italian

---

✳ Village hotel, Olivone ✳

Albergo Olivone e Posta

Strictly for the sporty. This pink and white hotel has comfortable rooms for walkers and skiers above a busy café-restaurant that serves country fare such as rabbit terrine, local snails, lamb with basil and *gnocchi* with Gorgonzola cheese.

❖ 6718 Olivone TI **Tel** (091) 8721366 **Fax** (091) 8721687 **Meals** breakfast, lunch, dinner, snacks **Prices** rooms S-SS with breakfast **Rooms** 25, most have bath or shower, central heating, phone, TV, radio **Credit cards** AE, DC, MC, V **Closed** Jan **Languages** English, French, German, Italian

Index of hotel names

In this index, hotels are arranged in order of the most distinctive part of their name; in many cases, other parts of the name are also given after the main part, but very common prefixes such as 'Hotel', 'Gasthof' and 'Le' are omitted.

Index of hotel names

Index of hotel names

Index of hotel locations

In this index, hotels are arranged by the name of city, town or village they are in or near. Where a hotel is located in a very small place, it may also be indexed under a nearby place which is more easily found on maps.

Index of hotel locations

Index of hotel locations